D1242170

FOUNDATIONS OF MUSIC EDUCATION SERIES
Allen P. Britton, Editor

Prentice-Hall International, Inc., *London*
Prentice-Hall of Australia, Pty. Ltd., *Sydney*
Prentice-Hall of Canada, Ltd., *Toronto*
Prentice-Hall of India (Private) Ltd., *New Delhi*
Prentice-Hall of Japan, Inc., *Tokyo*

Teaching
Band Instruments
to Beginners

EMIL A. HOLZ

The University of Michigan

ROGER E. JACOBI

The University of Michigan
The Ann Arbor Public Schools

PRENTICE-HALL, INC., *Englewood Cliffs, New Jersey*

© 1966 by Prentice-Hall, Inc., Englewood Cliffs, New Jersey

Current printing (last digit)
10 9 8 7 6 5 4 3 2 1

All rights reserved. No part of this book may be reproduced in any form, by mimeograph or any other means, without permission in writing from the publishers.

Library of Congress Catalog Card Number: 66-22084

Printed in the United States of America

C-89202-P
C-89203-C

Foreword

The practical aim of the Foundations of Music Education Series is to provide music educators with a unified but highly flexible and completely authoritative treatment of the most important professional concerns. Individual books of the series may be combined in various ways to form complete textbooks for the wide variety of courses in music education offered by colleges and universities across the nation. On the other hand, each volume has been designed to stand alone as a definitive treatment of its particular subject area.

The pedagogical aim of the series is to present practical and proven techniques of successful teaching in compact and readable form for both college students preparing to teach and experienced teachers constantly searching for more efficient ways of thinking and teaching. The highest musical ideals must be accompanied by the greatest amount of practical common sense if music instruction is to be most successful.

The aesthetic aim of the series is to emphasize the purely musical values that must be realized in any program of music instruction if that program is to achieve ends worthy of the time and effort required to carry it on. In short, each of these works assumes first of all that music must be true to itself if it is to continue to hold a respected place in American education. The most telling criticisms made of the school music program in recent years, almost all of which have dealt largely with alleged aesthetic failings, have written this lesson in letters large enough for all to read.

Last, having pointed out the unifying concepts that underlie the works in this series, it is perhaps equally important to emphasize that each of the authors has written the book that he wanted to write, the book that he believed would be of most value to the profession. The series encompasses the individual convictions of a great variety of the most highly competent and experienced music educators. On their behalf as well as on my own, may I express the hope that it will contribute in a practical way to the improvement of music teaching.

ALLEN P. BRITTON,

EDITOR

Preface

This book was planned for college methods classes preceding or accompanying directed teaching in instrumental music. The authors have taught such courses and supervised the work of student teachers for many years. They have also been teachers in the public schools. This book discusses the methods they have found most successful in their own teaching and in the teaching of the many teachers they have known through contacts as departmental chairmen, clinicians, adjudicators, and consultants.

The authors believe that it is the intelligence and musicality of the individual musician that produces artistic performance in secondary school and college bands. Consequently, throughout this book they have insisted on the importance of creating a teaching-learning situation hospitable to the development of individual musicianship and mastery of the intellectual content of instrumental musical performance.

Detailed information about the teaching of the several band instruments has not been included. The student is encouraged to make full use of the bibliography, paying particular attention to books that discuss instruments with which he is not familiar. College classes will benefit if readings from this book and from those listed in the bibliography can be augmented by demonstrations in the classroom and by observations of instrumental music class teaching in elementary schools.

The authors have found great pleasure and satisfaction in teaching young children about music through the medium of the beginning band class. They hope that this book will help young teachers to acquire attitudes and techniques that will lead them to comparable pleasures and satisfactions.

Emil A. Holz
Roger E. Jacobi

Contents

1

A Brief
History of the School
Band Movement

Ensembles of wind and percussion instruments, commonly known as bands, have played an important part in America's musical life since Colonial times. However, bands came to form part of the musical life of elementary and secondary schools only during the first quarter of the twentieth century.

Vocal music had been established in the grammar schools of Boston by Lowell Mason in 1838, and his success had stimulated similar efforts in most of the larger cities of the land within two decades. By the end of the century, vocal music was firmly entrenched in elementary schools, and efforts were being made, with some success, to gain scholastic credit for high school choirs. The introduction of instrumental music had to wait for certain changes in the social and educational climate of the United States.

THE TOWN BAND
TRADITION

Before the American Revolution most bands in the colonies were attached to military units; these bands persisted after the war as military or town bands. Their instrumentation in the 1820's included perhaps eight reed instruments, five or six brass instruments, and a drum.

In the 1840's Adolphe Saxe effected improvements on the valve system of existing conical-bore, cup-mouthpiece brass instruments to produce a unified family of saxhorns ranging downward from the soprano fluegelhorn through the alto horn, tenor horn, and baritone to the tuba. The saxhorns were immediately popular in America because they had a common fingering system, were comparatively easy to master, and had more volume than the reed instruments. Within a decade the brass band, composed entirely of saxhorns, had replaced the older reed band.

The brass band tradition continued until well after the turn of the century in thousands of village "silver cornet bands." The tradition first came under attack in the 1870's because of the influence of Patrick Sarsfield Gilmore, a professional brass band leader, who became a specialist in the "spectacular." After creating successes in staging gigantic musical jubilees in New Orleans and Boston, Gilmore produced the World Peace Jubilee of 1872 in Boston. The chorus numbered 20,000, and the band and orchestra required 2,000 musicians. In addition—and more important to the history of the American band—Gilmore brought to America some of the outstanding European bands. These bands were considered finer than American bands, partly because of the large number of reed instruments they used.

When Gilmore became director of the 22nd Regiment Band of New York in 1873, he immediately reorganized it after the European fashion, developing within the short span of five years the prototype of the concert band as it has since been known in America. After Gilmore's death in 1892 his musicians were led by Victor Herbert for four years. This group was then dissolved, many of the men finding employment in a new band led by John Philip Sousa. Sousa, who had been director of the United States Marine Band, attracted such fine musicians and had such impeccable standards of performance and programming that he soon had the finest professional concert band America had known. His nationwide tours engendered such enthusiasm that village bands began to include reed instruments again. Sousa's success inspired the organization of many other "business bands," notably those of Alessandro Liberati, T. P. Brooks, Arthur Pryor, Frederick Neil Innes, Patrick Conway, and Bohumir Kryl. In the last decade of the nineteenth century there were well over 10,000 professional and amateur bands in the United States. Yet, by the end of World War I they had all but disappeared.

A number of factors led to the decline of professional and town bands. For years these bands had played both for listening and for dancing; thus the members enjoyed double opportunities for employment, especially at resorts and amusement parks. With the advent of jazz, the silver cornet band succumbed to the onslaught of saxophone and trumpet, for men accustomed to polkas, schottisches, waltzes, mazurkas, and two-steps, with perhaps a bit of ragtime, were unable to play jazz as excitingly as men who had had little other musical experience. Furthermore, amusement parks, dependent upon public transportation by street car, declined as traction companies lost out in competition with the more convenient automobile. The severe social and economic dislocations of World War I led to discontinuance of many town bands, although the military forces used bands at every level of operation. By the middle of the great depression of the 1930's only a handful of town bands were still active, and the professional touring band was but a memory.

THE GROWTH OF THE PUBLIC HIGH SCHOOL

In the early years of the nineteenth century, Latin schools, copied after European models, had been found inadequate for the needs of American society and had been gradually displaced by privately-operated academies and technical schools. By 1840 many school districts had purchased existing academies or created similar schools to provide free non-sectarian instruction for the graduates of publicly supported grammar schools. The number of new schools, called "high schools," grew to about 40 by 1860, 2,500 by 1880, and over 6,000 by 1890. (There were 29,479 public and parochial secondary schools in the United States in 1962!) [1]

At first the high schools tended to combine the characteristics of the academy and the technical school in order to provide a utilitarian type of training in addition to classical training. By 1885, however, the curriculum had become almost as rigidly classical as that of the early academies, and it was not until the last few years of the century that "practical" subjects reappeared. The high school curriculum of 1890 was almost entirely devoted to Latin, Greek, French, German, algebra, geometry, physics, chemistry, and history. In the ensuing decade courses in science, psychology, rhetoric, English literature, and civil government were added. By 1910 many schools were offering work in agriculture and home economics.

Under the impact of America's rapidly increasing industrialization and urbanization, the curriculum expanded greatly in the early years of

[1] E. V. Laughlin, "The Evolution of the American High School," *Education*, XXXV (March 1915), 446-447; and *Statistical Abstracts of the United States, 1965*, U. S. Department of Commerce (Washington, D.C.: U. S. Government Printing Office, 1965), p. 106.

the twentieth century. So did the *extra*-curriculum. Skills formerly learned by apprenticeship or by helping around farm and home began to be taught in schools. Responding to the needs of their communities, schools undertook many responsibilities formerly considered exclusively in the province of the home. Child health centers, child guidance clinics, hot lunch programs, school nurses, and supervised vacation playgrounds all appeared for the first time between 1890 and 1910. During the same period public high school enrollments grew from 202,963 in 1890, to 519,151 in 1910 (15,194,584 in 1964!).[2] The presence of more children, and of children of more widely varied backgrounds, led to a proliferation of subjects, the number of courses taught in high schools increasing by more than 250 per cent from 1890 to 1910. The "learning by doing" precepts of John Dewey, the first platoon schools, and the first junior high schools also date from this period.

Interscholastic athletic contests assumed a larger place in American life during these years. Both elementary and secondary schools began to institute play activities, and by the beginning of World War I, military training had been established in at least 82 high schools.

Concurrently, community agencies were being created to provide worthwhile activities for children whose non-school time had formerly been taken up by chores. The National Recreation Association, organized in 1906, had fostered the formation of public playgrounds in 180 cities by 1910. The Boy Scouts and the Girl Scouts were organized in America in 1910 and 1912. America was entering upon a period in which "all work and no play" in school could be replaced by William Wirt's motto for the "school city" of Gary, Indiana—"Work, study, play."

As the school sought to duplicate community life within its walls (even to student newspapers and governments), the firehouse band moved into the school-house, just as did the singing school in 1838.

INSTRUMENTAL MUSIC
COMES TO SCHOOL

Although instrumental music had no place in the secondary school curriculum in the 1800's, sporadic attempts to establish bands or orchestras were made even before the Civil War; the Boston Farm and Trades School had a band in 1857, for

[2] Hornell Hart, "Changing Social Attitudes and Interests," in *Recent Social Trends in the United States* (Report of the President's Research Council on Social Trends, one-volume edition; New York: Whittlesey House, 1934), p. 338; and Carol Joy Hobson and Samuel Schloss, *Fall 1964 Statistics of Public Elementary and Secondary Schools*, U. S. Department of Health, Education, and Welfare (Washington, D.C.: U. S. Government Printing Office, 1965), p. 9.

example. But high school bands and orchestras, where they existed at all before 1900, were small in size and woefully inadequate in instrumentation and musicianship. Most had arisen spontaneously upon the accidental coincidence of a few trained students and an interested leader.

However, numerous "kid bands," often organized by town bandsmen, were formed in the last quarter of the century. They sometimes rehearsed in school buildings, but were rarely conducted by school teachers. Their fortunes and those of school bands were precarious. Without a reservoir of trained students to fill vacancies, no band could perpetuate itself. Furthermore, the existence of a band as a part of the extra-curriculum made it difficult to enforce high standards of performance and to resist pressures from other activities. A study of high school yearbooks and similar records reveals a steadily recurring theme: "Our school organized its first band this year" in entries every three or four years. Orchestras seem to have been more permanent, probably because orchestral music was supposed to be more "educational" and because other elements of the community (lodges, factories, Boy Scout troops, etc.) offered band experience to those who sought it.

In some communities, where athletic programs were popular, "pep bands" were organized and developed into school bands. In others, music supervisors started bands to provide a musical activity for boys who could not, or would not, sing. A generation earlier, these boys would not have been in school at all. For them, a school band became a sort of club, with masculine activity (violent in a sense) that was ego-satisfying and socially acceptable. Sometimes teachers of science, or shop, or business arithmetic would organize bands because they knew what a band could do for boys with too much time to waste. Where military training had been established, ROTC and Junior Cadet bands flourished. And, inevitably, many bands were started by band instrument salesmen seeking a new market.

Some of the early school band directors were fine musicians, but too often they knew only their own instruments. Brute strength, endless repetition and sheer rote learning were often the only methods they had at their command. The repertoire, an easier version of the town band repertoire, usually consisted of a set of quickstep marches, a march-size book of waltzes and "overtures," with an occasional stimulating arrangement of a ragtime or blues hit. The customary procedure was to assemble a group of boys, pass out instruments, show each lad how to pucker and say "too," run over the fingering chart quickly (taking care not to mention alternate fingerings), and then to hope for the best. If the boys met often enough, sooner or later the results would begin to resemble music. Even with all these handicaps, many band directors, particularly in towns with good professional instructors, managed to make fine music. The general level, however, was undoubtedly very low until competition, spectacle, and new instructional methods were introduced.

SPECTACLES AND ORGANIZATIONS SPUR INTEREST

As the number of permanently established school bands began to grow (to between perhaps 350 and 400 by 1923), competitions began to be held. The brass and reed bands of the previous century had participated in competitive events throughout the nation, so the introduction of the band contest into a school life that already enjoyed competitive athletics and debating was natural. By the early 1920's a number of states had inaugurated some sort of band contest.

The first contest for school bands that came close to being national in scope was held in Chicago in 1923 as a part of the entertainment and promotion of a convention of the Music Industries Chamber of Commerce. The event attracted thirty school bands from thirteen states, the bands ranging in size from the twenty-five boys from Paw Paw, Michigan, to the seventy or more from each high school in Gary, Indiana. This hastily organized contest was a great success. Newspapers throughout the country printed stories about it, reporting that "music is fun," and that "jazz bands are getting jazzier," and that some bands included girls. Nevertheless, dissatisfaction among directors was intense, and it was apparent that such an event could not be continued under commercial sponsorship. As a result, immediately after the tournament (as it was called), C. M. Tremaine, secretary of the National Bureau for the Advancement of Music, was asked to reorganize the contest so that control would be held by the schools and the directors.

The National Bureau for the Advancement of Music was an industry-supported organization fostering music weeks, piano classes, music appreciation activities, and music memory contests. Through Tremaine's efforts the Bureau had cooperated closely with the Music Supervisors National Conference (now the Music Educators National Conference). The Conference, organized in 1907, had been primarily for music supervisors and teachers of vocal music in schools. Instrumental music teachers had begun to be very active from about 1916 and had fostered the establishment in 1922 of a Committee on Instrumental Affairs. Tremaine persuaded the committee to assume the supervision of future national band contests.

Rigorous standards for instrumentation, repertoire, and performance were set up, and provisions for equal representation for all sections of the country were devised. So severe were the new rules that not until 1926 were there enough qualified bands to enable the first "official" national contest to be held, although there were a number of state and regional contests under the new regulations in the intervening years. The 1926 contest, held at Fostoria, Ohio, stimulated the founding of the National School Band Association, which thereafter supervised the contests. The Conference continued as the parent body and the band instrument manufacturers, through the National Bureau, provided financial backing. Working closely, if not always agreeably, these groups and their representatives revised the instrumentation of the school band until it more closely matched that of Gilmore's or Sousa's professional bands or A. Austin Harding's University of Illinois band. Repertoire and performance standards were elevated and the traditional numerical scoring system was replaced by the Kansas system of divisional ratings.

The contests spurred other activities. In the next ten years, Hollis Dann assembled three national high school choruses, Joseph E. Maddy created the first of several national high school orchestras in 1926 and founded the National Music Camp at Interlochen, Michigan, in 1928. National orchestra and national solo competitions started in 1929. Ensemble contests at the national level began in 1934, and the first national contest for school vocal groups was held in 1936. In the meantime the national band contests grew phenomenally. So large did they become that after 1934 bands and orchestras had to hold national competitions in alternate years. In 1937 there were so many qualified groups that the "national" contests were held in ten regions to allow all the state band and orchestra winners to compete. Not until the travel restrictions of World War II caused the cancellation of the 1941 contest did national or regional competitions disappear.

These spectacular events so stimulated the American public that the contest grew from thirty bands in 1923 (with perhaps 1,400 students) to 1,949 schools and 57,373 students in the regional competitions of 1940. In the preliminary district and state events of the 1940 national finals, some 10,000 bands, orchestras, and choruses participated. In addition, there were 7,500 instrumental and vocal ensembles and over 15,000 instrumental soloists.[3]

The ferment created by contests helped to secure band instruction as almost universal in American schools. Band directors who had learned their trade in the many service bands of World War I were available and eager to teach in the public schools. Musicians who lost jobs because of the decline of music in parks, restaurants, and theaters sought positions

[3] *National School Music Competition-Festivals, 1940 Reports* (Chicago: National School Band, Orchestra and Vocal Associations, 1940), p. 5.

of security in the schools. Children with band training were inspired to continue in college, and some hoped to make school band directing their vocations. Colleges responded by creating new courses and curriculums for them. So great was the interest in school bands that the rigors of the great depression and the effects of World War II did not prevent the steady rise in their growth and quality.

2

The Rise
of Class Instruction
in Instrumental Music

In the years immediately preceding World War I a number of schools organized grade school bands. One of the most famous, the Joliet (Illinois) Grammar School Band, was founded in 1912 by J. M. Thompson, supervisor of music. Thompson induced his board of education to provide a set of instruments and then asked the sixth-grade teachers of the city to choose the two most intelligent boys in each of the twelve elementary schools. He reported to the Music Supervisors National Conference in 1916: "We had four trombones, two baritones, five cornets, etc. We told the boys we couldn't have a band entirely of cornets or clarinets, but I wanted each one to love his instrument. I said, 'Boys, I want you to love your horns'; and it was a case of love at first sight. I had a trombone instructor who took the four boys into one room; and an instructor on the clarinet who took the boys with clarinets into another room and then my chief man was an old bandmaster and in five weeks they were playing a march." [1]

[1] *Proceedings of the Music Supervisors National Conference* (1916), pp. 34-35. The Joliet High School Band was organized later in 1912 by A. R. McAllister upon the suggestion of J. Stanley Brown, Superintendent of Schools, who had heard the Rockford (Illinois) high school band play at a football game.

At about this same time Glenn H. Woods persuaded the board of education of Oakland, California, to provide $5,000 for the purchase of instruments and to employ a teacher to give free ensemble instruction in the city's schools. Professional teachers were engaged to give private lessons at reduced fees in the grammar schools. Woods told the Conference in 1914 that his city boasted nine bands and three orchestras in the high schools and twenty-two bands and nine orchestras in the grammar schools. Other successful grade school music programs were instituted in Rochester, New York, in 1918 and in Richmond, Indiana, in 1920 by Joseph E. Maddy.

THE MAIDSTONE MOVEMENT
AND THE VIOLIN CLASS

In 1908, Charles Farnsworth, then professor of music at Teachers College, Columbia University, reported the result of a remarkable experiment begun a few years earlier in the English town of Maidstone. A curate of the local church had inaugurated violin instruction for parish children, teaching them in groups. An enterprising music dealer had been quick to offer promotional materials, low-cost instruments, and instructors to any community that wished to emulate Maidstone. The movement swept England and culminated in a series of spectacular concerts at London's Crystal Palace, where several thousand children performed together, accompanied by a military band and a mammoth pipe organ.

Farnsworth's report was read by Albert G. Mitchell, a violinist of Dorchester, Massachusetts, who also served as supervisor of music in the public schools of Boston. Securing a leave for the winter of 1910-11, he went to England to observe the new teaching technique. On his return he started classes in Dorchester and helped others to organize violin classes in New England schools.

While Mitchell was experimenting with class instruction, after-school violin classes were being established in a number of cities. These classes were usually taught by professional studio teachers who agreed to meet groups of four to six students. Each child paid a share of the teacher's normal hourly fee, thus reducing the cost of instruction to a minimum, especially when local school boards could be induced to subsidize the project. That the violin class was given preference at this time seems to have been due to the inexpensiveness of the instrument—a complete outfit could be purchased for less than $20.

Since the teachers were studio teachers, they tried to use the same kinds of materials and methods in classes as they had with private students. This material was often uninteresting to the children attracted to the classes. The teachers also had had no experience with *groups* of beginners and tended to operate their classes on the pattern of master classes for advanced players. Consequently, their efforts were often unsuccessful and the fact of their failure was often made to represent the faultiness of the idea. However, Mitchell and a number of others, particularly Benjamin F. Stuber, persisted in trying to solve the problem of class instruction in instrumental music. At the same time Thaddeus P. Giddings, Hazel Gertrude Kinscella, W. Otto Miessner, and others were striving to create techniques for class instruction in piano. These pioneers felt that the solution lay in the creation of suitable materials, special teaching techniques, and dedicated teaching.

Working independently, but with some exchange of ideas, Mitchell and Stuber sought answers. The first problem was one of mechanics—how could a student learn correct bowings and finger positions if he had only a fraction of a lesson each week? Mitchell found that fingering charts and dummy violins would work. Pasting the charts on the dummy finger-boards and on the fingerboards of real violins, with replicas suspended before the class, he would point to the correct position, naming the pitch, and sounding it upon the piano until his students could associate pitch, position, and name. Bowing techniques were acquired by practice on dummy violins fitted with a channel between "bridge" and "fingerboard" through which the bow could be drawn only in a straight line.

The second problem was that of musical material—how could students be kept interested in the violin class during the necessary period of mechanical drill? Stuber found that his students worked best when he used melodic materials—simple songs and drills masquerading as songs. The interest of the child was discovered to be primarily in the melodic aspect of music. While the child was struggling with bowing on the open strings his teacher sounded chords at the piano to provide a sense of musical movement.

The third problem, and perhaps the most difficult, was that of class management—how could students of varying abilities and interests be kept at the necessary tasks so that the work might proceed efficiently? This problem was solved in part by the use of melodic materials and by the provision of alternate parts. The class situation was found to stimulate competition that helped maintain discipline and interest. Frequent per-formance was also found to be beneficial.

As experience accumulated, the pioneers of the violin class movement organized their materials and ideas into instruction books. The first two widely disseminated methods for violin classes were Mitchell's *Violin Class Method* (Boston: Oliver Ditson Company, 1924) and Stuber's *Instrumental Music Course* (Chicago: E. T. Root & Sons, 1923; later published by The Raymond T. Hoffman Company of Chicago as *The Melody Way Method*).

THE EMERGENCE OF HETEROGENEOUS METHOD

The men and women working with the new class teaching techniques exchanged ideas with each other and with other teachers through professional associations and the columns of educational periodicals. Their enthusiasm inspired others to follow their example. Most of these teachers found that they had first to teach themselves to play all the instruments. Professional musicians, fearful of competition for jobs and students, refused to divulge their secrets, and manufacturers of band instruments, guarding their trade secrets, sometimes withheld information. So they worked alone, observing professionals when they could, experimenting with embouchure formation, and trying out their methods in their classes. Stuber was particularly successful and was able to enroll large numbers of students in instrumental music classes in Akron, Ohio, where he supervised a large staff of teachers in the public schools.

In 1923 Joseph E. Maddy and Thaddeus P. Giddings brought out the first heterogeneous class method that made use of all that had been learned in the first decade of instrumental class instruction. *The Universal Teacher* (Elkhart, Indiana: C. G. Conn, Ltd., later assigned to The Willis Music Company of Cincinnati) was almost entirely melodic. No scale exercises or drill materials were used. Students were asked to sing first, then play, finding for themselves the fingerings that made the tunes sound right. From the first, tunes were transposed by ear so that experience in the full chromatic possibilities of the beginner's range was available, and sharps and flats were no more difficult than naturals. The last several pages of the method were devoted to three-part harmonizations, each part appearing in all books so that children could experience harmony as well as melody.

The Universal Teacher opened up a whole new world of possibilities. No longer would a child need to practice for months before he could play his first tune; no longer were players of "harmony" instruments limited to accompaniment rhythms within a restricted range; no longer would a child be expected to know musical "facts" he could not use in his own daily practice. Because the material was so simple, and because the method depended upon the learner finding the answers, the instruction could be, and often was, supervised by classroom teachers with no musical training beyond the minimum included in the normal school curriculum of the day. Classes were even taught successfully by radio! While the method did not try to do as much as the older studio methods, it enabled more children than ever before to study instrumental music and influenced the writing of many other instrumental class method books.

A large number of class methods especially designed for use in elementary schools appeared during the 1930's. Some followed the lead of the pioneers and used the tuneful approach. Others devoted most of their pages to drill material. By 1940 a wide variety of materials was available to the teacher of elementary instrumental music. He could find almost any approach he wished to use—melodic, chordal, diatonic, chromatic, rhythmic, heterogeneous, homogeneous, or "wholesale." The most successful methods seem to have combined the best features of the melodic approach with those of the drill approach, supported by sound pedagogical organization. Of the dozens of method books that appeared in the first forty years of heterogeneous wind class teaching, the following have perhaps been most significant, either because of their contributions to the development of a pedagogy or because of their great popularity among instrumental music teachers.

The Universal Teacher, by Joseph E. Maddy and Thaddeus P. Giddings (Cincinnati: The Willis Music Company, 1926).

The World of Music Band Course, by William D. Revelli, Victor L. F. Rebmann, Charles B. Righter, and G. E. Holmes (Chicago: Ginn and Company, 1939).

Easy Steps to the Band, by Maurice D. Taylor (New York: Mills Music, Inc., 1942).

Belwin Elementary Band Method, by Fred Weber (New York: Belwin, Inc., 1945).

The Basic Method for Beginning Band, by Dale C. Harris and Fred Wiest (New York: Educational Music Service, Inc., 1957).

First Division Band Course, by Fred Weber and others (Rockville Centre, L.I., N.Y.: Belwin, Inc., 1962).

3

Introducing
Instrumental Music
to the Curriculum

Programs of instruction in instrumental music already exist in most school districts in the United States. However, many are instituted yearly, not only in countless dozens of new schools built to serve the expanding population, but also in long-established schools hitherto without such instruction. The institution and development of new programs requires that certain steps be taken if the program is to flourish.

Ideally, these steps will have been taken by the administration and patrons before an instructor is engaged. When such is not the case, the new teacher must initiate the process.

FORMULATING
A COURSE OF ACTION

To begin, leadership is essential. It might be provided by the superintendent, a principal or teacher, a member of the board, a parent, or a music dealer. Professional educators might be more likely to act because of a belief that the general education of students would benefit. Supporters of interscholastic athletics or community "boosters" might hope for a band to serve the community in several ways. Music dealers might be motivated by personal gain or, just as easily, by the same public and educational concerns held by the others.

Once the idea has been planted, the superintendent or his delegated staff should appoint a study committee to investigate all aspects of the proposal. The committee should be small enough to insure effective operation yet include a variety of people representing many interests. All should be interested in music and somewhat knowledgeable about it. They should have leadership qualities, for part of their work will be to interpret their recommendations to the community segments they represent. The committee might include the instrumental and vocal music teachers (whose training and contacts are the best immediate source of information to the committee), an elementary school principal, a classroom teacher, a parent of a child who already plays an instrument, and one or more persons from the community. In addition, the district would be wise to secure the services of an outside consultant from a nearby college or university.

If for one reason or another a study committee has not been formed, the teacher charged with the responsibility of establishing the program should constitute himself a committee of one to make an equally thorough study. He should develop his entire plan and have it approved by the school administration and the board before a single student receives instruction on an instrument. This recommendation seems idealistic and time-consuming. Perhaps it is; but idealism is no fault, and time may be spent as easily going in the right direction as in the wrong.

The study committee will need to discuss these questions:

1. What are to be the goals of the instrumental music program?
2. How is the program to be financed?
3. Who will be enrolled in the program?
4. How will instruments be supplied?
5. Where and when will classes be taught?
6. How can administrative and public support be maintained?

THE GOALS OF THE INSTRUMENTAL MUSIC PROGRAM

Hopefully the study committee will first discuss the goals of the program they expect to institute. The question is fundamental and must be faced directly and honestly. Without proper goals the program can wander aimlessly or move in an unfortunate direction to the detriment of the children involved. The committee will need to ask: Is the goal merely to establish a high school band; or is it to provide children with artistic experience through which they may develop a love and understanding of music? Are the students to be exploited by school and community; or is music to be studied as seriously as other subjects, and will performance pressures be reduced to make this possible?

Once the goals have been defined they should be codified in a statement of philosophy. Help in writing the statement may be obtained by reading in the professional literature of music education or by studying curriculum guides from schools with excellent music programs.[1] The finished statement might well be similar to this one:

Music has become an integral part of the life of the American child—in school, at home, and in the community. Great philosophers and educators of all time have recognized its importance in education, but most eras and most parts of the world have made it available only to children from families of favorable economic status. It remained for the American public to demand music for all children. Out of this demand has come increasing attention to the study of music as a fundamental part of the school curriculum. The primary purpose of all music education is the development of a love and appreciation of music.

Music can contribute to the physical, intellectual, social, and spiritual growth of the child. Through varied experiences such as singing, rhythmic movement, creative activities, listening, and playing on instruments, each child can discover and develop his own ability and interest in music. The pleasure of making music not only affords a means of self-expression, but also helps the child adjust more effectively to the society in which he lives. Our basic philosophy is that such opportunity should be provided for every child in our school system. Music is a universal language, and it is the fervent hope of this school system that all children will understand, enjoy, and use this language.

FINANCING THE INSTRUMENTAL MUSIC PROGRAM

Instrumental music requires adequate financial support. It is not necessarily more expensive than other areas of instruction, but it does demand a considerable outlay of funds at the beginning, and regular purchases of many kinds of equipment as the program grows. The first consideration is the availability of sufficient funds to pay a *competent* teacher. When unqualified persons are hired,

[1] The U. S. Department of Health, Education, and Welfare publishes *Music Curriculum Guides,* identifying schools that have made their guides available.

the program is often doomed to failure. Instruction is poor, children are cheated, the taxpayers' money is wasted, and the time invested in starting the program is lost. A school is far better off without an instrumental music program if it can only afford a poor one.

Other financial considerations have to do with sources of funds for music, instruments, equipment, and, perhaps, uniforms. Ideally, if instrumental music is to have a place in the curriculum all costs should be borne by tax funds. Some school districts cannot assume the entire burden. They therefore take as much of the load as they can and hope that the community will provide the balance. A clear understanding of this problem and its answers at the beginning of the organizational process can prevent the exploitation of students and their parents by unnecessary tag days, ice cream socials, usage fees, and other schemes.

A new teacher, or a teacher new to a district, would do well to investigate the matter of finances as soon as possible. He should seek information from the superintendent, the business manager, and the principals. Some school systems allocate funds directly to the music department to be spent as needed throughout the system. Others allocate funds to individual schools for distribution by the principals in accordance with their estimates of departmental needs. Whatever the formula, the teacher usually has a chance to request funds for his work. Budgets are prepared a year in advance by individual schools or departments, submitted to the superintendent's office, and reviewed. The anticipated expenditures are compared with the anticipated income. When anticipated costs are higher than anticipated income, the board may ask for more income by increasing taxation or it may reduce expenses until the budget is balanced. The teacher will need to keep a close watch on the parts of the budget that concern him and his work.

Sometimes communities reject taxation proposals. When they do, and when school districts must retrench, the instrumental music program should not be dropped from the elementary schools but cut back as equally as possible throughout the program. One or two years without a beginning program in the elementary schools destroys the foundation of the entire program. It is better to meet all classes only half as frequently than to meet only half the classes that should be taught.

WHO SHALL STUDY
INSTRUMENTAL MUSIC?

The study committee should consider whether the instrumental music program is to be open to all interested students or whether the number is to be restricted by some type of qualifying procedure. The decision may be made philosophically or practically. If there are many schools but few teachers, restrictions may be advisable so that those who do study will benefit. If the staff is large enough, it may be desirable to let every interested child participate in the beginning class.

Most beginning classes seem to be fifth-grade classes. Some teachers have found that they succeed as well by starting students in the sixth or seventh grades, particularly if classes meet frequently. Others prefer to start in the fourth grade and move more slowly. Decisions made in this regard will be influenced by the availability of teacher time and the conditions that prevail in the rest of the elementary school curriculum.

When a school introduces instrumental music for the very first time, students from grades five through seven should be encouraged to enroll in beginning classes in order to establish the total program as quickly as possible. Diligent students will be able to make significant progress and have an opportunity to play in major ensembles before they graduate. High school students often have too many scholastic and social responsibilities to enable them to do the necessary practicing.

THE SOURCE
OF INSTRUMENTS

The committee will need to determine whether parents will be expected to provide all the instruments, whether the school will work out a rental-purchase arrangement with a music store or rental company, or whether the school will purchase all instruments for the students to use with or without fee.

The program will be most likely to succeed if instruments can be placed in the hands of beginners at small expense to parents. This requires a proportionately larger investment by the district and is therefore not always feasible. Rental fees of $2 to $5 a semester can be charged for the first year of instruction. After that time, students who wish to continue can be required to buy their own instruments, so that the next class may have the same opportunities. Parents appreciate this plan because they need not buy an instrument until they know the child will benefit.

Many school systems make arrangements with a band instrument company or a local music store for students to rent instruments for a three-month trial period. After the trial period, the child and his parents decide about continuing. If the child continues, the rental fee is applied to the purchase of the instrument. If he does not, the instrument may be returned to the dealer, who then sells it as a used instrument.

Certain instruments are almost always purchased by the school— usually those that are so expensive that parents are unlikely to buy them and those needed for completing an acceptable instrumentation for the band or orchestra. If instruction on a majority of the instruments is to be offered in the elementary schools to insure full instrumentation in the secondary schools it is wise to purchase oboes, bassoons, French horns, baritones, tubas, bass drums (with stands), snare drums (with stands), violas, cellos, and string basses.

Many schools use only "basic" instruments (flute, clarinet, cornet, trombone, violin, and cello) in the elementary schools, transferring some students to the less common and more expensive instruments in the junior high school. When this system is used, each elementary school should provide cellos, a snare drum, and a bass drum (with stands).

TEACHING STATIONS
AND SCHEDULING

The availability of teaching stations for instrumental music must not be overlooked. Many a promising program has foundered because facilities were inadequate. Although they need not be specially designed, instrumental music rooms in elementary schools should be acceptable acoustically and separated from other rooms so that regular class work will not be disturbed.

The committee will need to recommend the way in which instrumental music is to be scheduled—during the regular hours of school or before and after school. The problems of releasing students from classes and the amount of interference with other activities merit consideration. If classes are to meet during school hours, either the school schedule must be modified or the music classes rotated so that no student misses too much of his regular class work. The number of class meetings a week, the duration of the classes, the size of classes, ability groupings, and the homogeneity or heterogeneity of the classes must be studied carefully. The schedule for instrumental music in the elementary school will be determined in part by the total responsibilities of the teacher, who may be assigned to other elementary and secondary schools. Since all decisions on scheduling will eventually be made by principals and other administrators, committee recommendations should reflect an understanding of administrators' concerns.

PUBLICIZING
THE NEW PROGRAM

After recommendations have been drawn up, the study committee should explain the proposed program to the board of education, the teaching staff, and the community. Proper support is usually obtainable if the information is presented effectively. A carefully prepared report, outlining the problems and explaining the committee's recommendations, should be made formally to the board of education and the staff. Dissemination of information through public news media is recommended.

A teacher who has done the study without the help of a committee should follow the same procedure. His well-written plan will be of inestimable help in the development of enthusiasm for the work he hopes to do.

4

Recruiting
a New Class

Ever since 1923, when Karl Gerhkens invented it, a popular motto of school music teachers has been "Music for Every Child—Every Child *for* Music." In the elementary schools and junior high schools, vocal and general music teachers have implemented the motto with programs that have sought to provide every child with the opportunity to learn music and to make intelligent choices concerning it. The cost of instruments and the highly specialized nature of instrumental music has prevented instrumental music teachers from offering instruction to all children at all grade levels. However, the young listener has been well served through the performances of school bands and orchestras.

Experience in playing band and orchestra instruments should be made available to all students who wish to learn. The exclusion of children of average talents and economic status, or of below-average academic achievement, is undemocratic and has no place in tax-supported American schools. Although development of outstanding performing groups is essential, for only in such groups can the most talented students have experiences commensurate with their abilities, the neglect of those who cannot contribute to prestigious bands or orchestras negates the fundamental principles of all public education.

The goal of music instruction in the public schools is to provide for every child an opportunity to learn to love and to understand music. Some children will not take advantage of the opportunity, but it must be extended. For many children, the approach to music through an instrument is more effective than any other. For some, the study of an instrument deepens and broadens interests and understandings acquired through vocal music or the general music class. Probably every child, who at some time in his life wants to play a musical instrument, should have the chance.

The rate of drop-out need cause no more concern than the attrition of student mathematicians, scientists, poets, or athletes. Students make choices, and one of the functions of a public school system in a democratic society is to enable intelligent selection of interests and activities based upon experience. Students who find other activities more interesting or more suited to their abilities will drop out of instrumental music, of course. But they will have learned much about music in the meantime. Those whose interests and talents are keenest will continue, some to become connoisseurs of music, others to become the teachers and performers of the next generation.

Some public schools provide instrumental music on an exploratory basis for every student. Instruments are demonstrated, and each child is taught a few notes on all of them. Several weeks are spent in exploring each instrument. At the end of the exploratory period teacher and child know which instrument is most suited to the child's interests and abilities. Some children, completely uninterested in music, probably would not benefit from such an experience and should not participate.

If it is impossible to offer exploratory instruction to all children, efforts should be made to provide the opportunity for all who wish it. This will require recruiting, demonstrating, and, perhaps, testing. It is not difficult to interest students in the possibility of learning to play a musical instrument if the presentation is carefully planned. The planning will need to include consideration of the status of instrumental music in the school system, the availability of instruments, and the selection and placement of students. These considerations will control the timing and content of the several parts of the recruiting process.

NOTIFICATION
TO PARENTS

Unless instrumental music has been firmly established in a school system, and unless the school supplies all the instruments needed in a beginning class, the first step in recruiting is to notify parents that classes in instrumental music are being organized. Parents should be told, in a dignified letter, of the nature of the offering and should be invited to attend a demonstration of instruments at an evening meeting in the school. The letter should be signed by the instrumental music teacher and an administrator. If the recruiting is being done on a city-wide basis, the superintendent should sign, although parents are frequently better acquainted with the name of the local principal. Provision for a response from parents, perhaps on a detachable portion of the letter to be returned by the child, will help greatly in planning the demonstration.

The letter should be very carefully prepared—neat, to the point, and free of misspelled words and faulty grammar. It should attempt to answer the general questions parents might ask: where and when the demonstration will be given and by whom; who may enroll in the new program; how parents can be assured that their children will benefit; and who can answer more specific inquiries. Interest in the demonstration can be stimulated by frequent reminders in the classrooms of the prospective students, encouraging them to talk among themselves and to their parents about the forthcoming demonstration.

If instrumental music has been firmly established and all instruments are provided by the school, this letter may not be needed. A demonstration of instruments to all interested students would be followed by a letter informing parents of the program and asking the return of an enrollment form if they wish to take advantage of the offering. A demonstration for parents is not essential in this case although a meeting to answer questions is highly recommended both for the edification of the parents and the strengthening of public relations.

THE DEMONSTRATION

The most crucial part of the recruiting phase of the instrumental music program is the demonstration of instruments. If it is well organized, interesting, and meaningful, it will do more to attract students and parents than any other device. At its best, the demonstration becomes an exciting musical experience for parents and children.

When the school must depend upon a commercial supplier of instruments, the approval of the superintendent of schools must be secured before the supplier's representative is invited to conduct a demonstration. If the permission is not forthcoming, the demonstration may be presented by the instrumental music teacher, with the help of colleagues or students, and the parents may be informed of the names and addresses of local dealers who can supply instruments.

Suppliers' representatives have developed demonstrations that are entertaining and meaningful to parents and children alike. They have worked closely with music teachers and are aware of the goals and standards that prevail. Their wide experience can be of great value to the young teacher in organizing a beginning program. They have devised informative talks, couched in language parents understand, with illustrations that appeal to children. Printed matter distributed by instrument companies answers many of the questions parents ask, and, since usually only one parent is able to attend an evening demonstration, the material helps the family reach an informed decision.

Dealers' displays are apt to be eye-catching, showing the instruments against bright red plush and highlighting them with clip-on spotlights so that the presentation is dramatic and spectacular. The salesman knows that he must be a showman—energetic, dynamic, understanding, and stimulating. He is, in every sense of the word, an actor. With jokes and clever manipulation of the instruments he commands the attention of his audience. He knows that he must make a strong impression so that every child and every parent in the room will remember his message during the family councils that follow the demonstration.

The teacher can emulate the salesman, and it is to his advantage to learn to do so. Too often children and parents are repelled, when they would otherwise be attracted, by a dull, monochromatic presentation replete with meaningless educational jargon. Throughout the recruiting process the teacher should remember that he is trying to persuade people to take time and money from other needs and desires in order to undertake a learning process that requires hard work toward remote goals. Selling work is never easy! It must be done with energy and understanding, dynamically, and with a flair.

When the demonstration is to be given by the instrumental music teacher, he should call upon his colleagues or students to help him present the various instruments unless he can play each of them very well. Children will be impressed not only by the size, shape, and color of an instrument but also by its sound. And, if the sound is good, the children will learn one of the goals toward which they are to aspire. Musical selections should be short and simple; a display of technical brilliance may make the prospect seem unattainable to the student and his parents.

A few basic concepts about music can be taught during the demonstration. The families of instruments should be introduced before the individual members of the families. The acoustical fact of the determination of pitch by the length of the vibrating body is easily shown as instruments are presented. The nature of musical tone as the result of regular vibrations and the nature of vibrating media are readily taught. Whenever possible, examples from the child's experience should be used. Every step of the process must be so organized that the audience is led from simple to complex in comprehensible steps.

The demonstration must start exactly on time and should never be long. The more quickly the teacher can cover the essential material entertainingly and informatively, the more likely he is to secure the attention and support of his audience. He should remember that refusal and rejection can become habitual and that opportunities to say "no" or to let the mind wander must be avoided. If he can keep his audience alert, he will find increasing interest in his theme, and more and more parents will wish to have their children enjoy this fascinating subject.

As a rule, children tend to prefer the popular instruments. A good demonstration cannot ignore these but should probably not overemphasize them. If there are foreseeable imbalances in instrumentation, a slight shift of emphasis in the demonstration will often help to equalize the choices of instruments. It is often advisable not to demonstrate the percussion instruments since they are so appealing to children but such a small part of the instrumentation of a band or orchestra.

A SUCCESSFUL
DEMONSTRATION

The following material is a demonstration "script" that has been used with great success in the elementary schools of Ann Arbor, Michigan. It has yielded instrumental class enrollments as high as 72.8 per cent of the total fifth grade enrollment in a school system that supplies rental instruments at moderate fees. The demonstration is presented to children during the first weeks of September each year.

Good morning, boys and girls. We are delighted to be with you today. On stage are several instrumental music teachers who teach in our schools. We are going to show and play a number of musical instruments.

Now that you are in the fifth grade you have the privilege of learning to play a musical instrument right here in school. I know you heard the school orchestra perform at school assemblies last year. And I am sure many of you remember way back when you were in kindergarten and came in to watch one of our rehearsals. Today we are going to tell you about these instruments and how you might be able to join one of our classes.

First, we are going to show you the instruments of the string family. Miss Jones, our string teacher, will show you these instruments.[1]

Miss Jones comes to the front of the stage and says:

Boys and girls, before I show you any of the stringed instruments I want to show you something I have in my hand. Can you see it? It's a rubber band. I'm sure you have all held a rubber band between your thumb and first finger, snapped it, and heard a sort of musical sound. Listen. Let us see if you can hear it. Did you? Good—some of you did. Now let me stretch the band around a partly-opened box, pluck it again, and see what happens. Listen! That was certainly louder, wasn't it? The violin I now have in my hand works very much the same way as the rubber band.

Miss Jones then demonstrates the violin, plucking and bowing the strings, and playing a short melody. She continues by demonstrating the other stringed instruments on which instruction will be given. Then she introduces Mr. Smith to demonstrate the woodwinds.

Mr. Smith begins by saying:

Boys and girls, you can see I have nothing in my hands. Now, let me reach inside my shirt pocket—and what do I find? A small, thin piece of wood. It is a reed, made from cane that comes all the way from France. I'm going to place the thin end in my mouth and blow my breath over it. Hmmm. Nothing happened, did it? Correct. Let me reach in my pocket and see what I can find. It's a mouthpiece! Watch and listen to what happens when I place the end of the reed and the mouthpiece in my mouth and blow again. My goodness, that certainly was a funny sound!

But do you know, it's pretty hard to hold this reed against the mouthpiece all the time. Let me reach into another pocket to see what I can find. Can you see this? It is made of metal and has two screws. We call it a ligature. Let's all say that word together—ligature. Good for you. Now, let's see. In my right coat pocket I have something else. It's made of wood and you can look through it when you hold it up to your eye. Raise your hand if you think you know the name of this. Let's see what this boy thinks it is—a tube? Well, yes. But it is a special kind of tube called a barrel joint. Now that you think of it, it does look a bit like a barrel, doesn't it?

Watch as I attach the barrel joint to the mouthpiece. There it is. When I play again, raise your right hand if you think the tone is higher. Listen carefully! You are a fine group of students. Most of you heard correctly—the tone was lower. Believe it or not, I have another piece to add. Here it is, in my inside coat pocket.

---

[1] Some school systems prefer to start string instruction one year earlier than wind and percussion instruction because it is believed that (1) strings are considered to be more difficult than band instruments and thus should be started earlier; (2) wind instrument students can play melodies rather early but string students should move more slowly in order to develop proper bowing habits essential to good string playing; and (3) great relaxation is required in string playing and can be achieved better at an earlier age.

Mr. Smith plays a few notes with the left-hand joint and then proceeds, by steps, to assemble the entire clarinet and to play a little tune. He demonstrates the other woodwind instruments without discussing their assembly but speaking about the different ways of tone production and the different kinds of reeds. He then introduces Mr. Johnson, the teacher of brass instruments.

Mr. Johnson also comes to the stage with no visible "props." He says:

Boys and girls, the instrument I have does not use strings or reeds to make vibrations. Instead, I use my own lips. Listen to the buzzing sound I can make with them. That doesn't sound much like music, does it? My instrument also uses a mouthpiece and I simply put it to my lips and buzz into it. That's louder, but not much prettier! But I can play melodies with just the mouthpiece.

Now I take my cornet, add the mouthpiece and play through it. So that you will understand the whole process, I will first buzz my lips, then keep the buzz going as I put the mouthpiece in place and then add the cornet. That's certainly much louder than the other instruments we've heard, isn't it?

The cornet is nothing more than a bugle with a few added gadgets. Without using my fingers I can play some bugle calls. I know you must be wondering how I make higher and lower sounds without changing the length of the instrument. I do it with my lips. Listen again as I change the sound from my lips. When I do that with the instrument I can play the notes of a bugle call.

But I can't play any songs this way. So I have to make the instrument longer to get lower notes. That is what the three valves are for. When I push one of them, the air goes through extra tubing and the tone is lower.

Mr. Johnson plays a melody, demonstrates the other brass instruments rather quickly and turns the program over to the chairman who tells the students how they may enroll in the class.

It is important to note that the entire presentation has been organized so that the students are participating in the learning process, that all steps are taken in a logical order, and that nothing is left unexplained once it has been introduced. The teachers' remarks are ordered to stimulate the curiosity of the children, and the emphasis has been on musical factors. Social implications, the promise of a place in the wonderful high school band, and the improvement of "culture" are omitted because they are inappropriate and misleading.

SELECTING, TESTING, ASSIGNING

At the close of the demonstration, parents should be given a chance to indicate their interest. A simple form may be devised by which the parents, after family discussion, can enroll their children in the class or request an appointment for further information. If instruments are provided by the school, the procedure is usually quite simple. If the parents are to rent or purchase instruments, time must be allowed to permit them to make the necessary arrangements and for the teacher to follow through; otherwise, there will be unfortunate delays in the organization of the class.

Many schools prefer to screen applicants for the beginning class before the demonstration so that only those who have indicated reasonable aptitude and interest will be involved. Other schools give tests after the demonstration, since students and parents are then more apt to make informed selections of instruments. Whenever the screening is done, it should consider intelligence and interest as well as musicality. Actually, most of the aptitude tests currently available from instrument companies are among the roughest of measuring devices. The more elaborate tests are too cumbersome for use in most schools. The best talent test continues to be experience in music. If the goal of the music department is to offer musical experience to as many as possible, a simple test is usually adequate. Students with high intelligence or interest should not be excluded from the program even though their music test scores might be low. Intelligence and interest are important in the study of music and can frequently overcome deficiencies in talent. The instructor would be wise to choose his students (if he *must* make choices) on the basis of a combination of indicators—talent test, school grades, interest and motivation, and recommendations from teachers and principals.

The testing should include an assessment of the student's physical capabilities for playing the instrument of his choice. If time permits, each student should be given a chance to produce a tone on his chosen instrument or on its mouthpiece. The instructor may then be able to advise parents if the formation of lips and teeth is appropriate. Length of arm, size of finger, and digital dexterity are also considerations for selecting some instruments. Whenever possible, the student should be permitted to undertake the instrument of his choice. When another instrument is suggested or recommended, the teacher must be very tactful in explaining his reasons.

The testing part of the recruiting process is another way by which the teacher can fix the attention of the students on instrumental music. While he is being tested, the child can not avoid thinking about the possibility of playing.

After testing, assessing, and consulting have been completed, the teacher notifies those students who have been admitted to the class and tells them what is expected at the first class meeting. The notice should be by letter to the parents so that they will be aware of their responsibilities in relation to practice schedules at home, care of instruments, class attendance, and other pertinent concerns.

THE USE OF
PRE-BAND INSTRUMENTS

Melody instruments of a flute-like character have enjoyed much popularity in elementary schools since their introduction in the 1930's. They have been employed as exploratory and talent-finding devices by instrumental music teachers and as enrichment devices by teachers of vocal and general music. The two uses have not always been compatible. When used as pre-band instruments, they have been said to expedite the learning of musical fundamentals, the development of finger coordination and dexterity, the training of the ear through rote playing, development of reading skills, and the identification of the most talented and eager children. In the vocal music program they have been said to help children realize pitch and notation relationships, distinguish intervals in part-singing, create melodies, and participate in music when voices were uncertain. The instrumentalist has used melody instruments in regularly scheduled classes; the vocalist or generalist has used them only as needed.

If pre-band instruments are used in the instrumental music program, instruction should be given by the teachers of instrumental music so that the learning is coordinated with the activities of the beginning class. Besides, classroom teachers and vocal music teachers have enough of their own work to do without being obligated to the instrumental music department. If melody instruments are used widely as part of the general music program, the instrumental music teacher should not intrude, since his goals may be quite different. On the other hand, when the general music program is weak or non-existent, the teaching of music through pre-band instruments can make a valuable contribution to the education of children.

If pre-band instruments are to be used as part of a talent-finding program preliminary to the selection of students for the instrumental music class, instruction should begin during the second semester of the fourth grade year or during the summer immediately following. This kind of scheduling permits the students to progress quite well on the pre-band instruments, at least to a point that enables the instrumental music teacher to make informed judgments about their chances of success. The classes may be taught to all fourth-grade students (probably needfully if scheduled during the school year) or to all those who desire the experience (probably best as a summer activity). The amount of time given to the use of pre-band instruments will depend to a great extent upon the availability of teacher time and the scheduling of other activities for fourth grade students. It is not recommended that pre-band instrument classes completely replace the general music classes. Some schools have solved this problem by teaching pre-band instruments intensively for a few weeks; others have limited pre-band instrument instruction to after-school hours.

Pre-band instruments have been used with considerable success in many schools. Other schools, with equally successful instrumental music programs, have not used pre-band instruments at all.

5

Scheduling Instrumental Music in Elementary Schools

One of the most vexing problems facing instrumental music teachers is the scheduling of classes in elementary schools.[1] In elementary schools, all classes compete on an equal basis for time in the school day. More and more classes are being crowded into an already tight schedule so that instrumental music must vie with conversational languages, physical education, general music, art, and the classes of special teachers of other subjects. The difficulties are increased by the presence of a number of other people providing special services (assistant principals, counselors, nurses, librarians, speech correctionists, psychometrists, and others) who need time and space to do their work. Furthermore, there is far more experimentation and differentiation in elementary schools than in secondary schools. Traditional systems, platoon schools, non-graded schools, team-teaching schools, and ability groupings within grade levels all make

[1] Scheduling at all levels is difficult, but the attention of most instrumental music teachers has been directed toward the solution of problems in the secondary schools—which may seem more important but are actually much easier to solve. In junior and senior high schools, to have a workable schedule, large ensemble classes that cut across grade-level lines are scheduled first, and the rest of the schedule is built around them.

31

special demands on the schedule. In a sense, all these factors have put instrumental music in a less secure position than it enjoyed in former years.

Fundamentally, the scheduling of instrumental music in elementary schools depends upon administrative support and financial resources. These determine the willingness of principals to make needed adjustments and the ability of administrators to provide enough teachers and teaching stations to enable a good program to be offered. In some systems, the scheduling will be done, at least for building and hourly assignments, by the supervisor or coordinator of music. In others, all the arrangements will have to be made by a single teacher.

SCHEDULING
SEVERAL SCHOOLS

Most school districts have several elementary schools of different sizes. The instrumental music teacher will want to provide classes in each of these schools and to arrange his schedule so that all children will receive approximately equal amounts of instructional time in classes of about the same size. He must first determine how many hours a week he can give to his work in the elementary schools. If he is wise, he will try not to neglect his beginning classes for the benefit of advanced groups, for he will know that his program can grow only in proportion to his success in meeting the needs of the largest number of students and that the elementary school program is the foundation upon which successful secondary programs are built.

Prescott and Chidester [2] discuss five kinds of instruction: (1) the wholesale method, with all instruments in one class; (2) the full band method; (3) classes of families of instruments (all woodwinds, all brasswinds, etc.); (4) classes of like instruments (classes for flutes, clarinets, cornets, etc.); and (5) private lessons. Private lessons are usually too expensive to consider. Classes of individual instruments are feasible if there is enough teacher time. The wholesale method is cheapest in terms of teacher time but the least likely to produce acceptable results—the compromises that must be made to meet the diverse demands of strings and winds create almost insurmountable problems.

In school districts without adequate financial support and teacher time for instrumental music, the elementary school schedule will have to

[2] Gerald R. Prescott and Lawrence W. Chidester, *Getting Results with School Bands* (New York: Carl Fischer, Inc., and Minneapolis: Paul A. Schmitt Music Co., 1938), p. 51.

be worked out within the limits of the time available, using whichever plan or combination of plans will best fit the situation. Where funds, teacher time, and administrative support permit, it is possible to create a schedule that equalizes the opportunities for children throughout the system. The plan set forth below provides an example of this kind of scheduling. It may be modified to meet particular needs.

The *first step* in the plan is to categorize the elementary schools by the number of classrooms furnishing instrumental music students. A small school, in this plan, would have only one fifth-grade classroom and one sixth-grade classroom. A medium-sized school would have three or four classrooms enrolling instrumental music students. A large school would have five or more such classrooms.

The *second step* is to determine what kinds of classes will be scheduled in each of the size groupings for the most efficient use of teacher time and the greatest benefit to the students. Generally speaking, classes of like instruments will be taught in the large schools, classes grouped by families in the medium-sized schools, and mixed classes (beginning band and beginning string classes) in the small schools.

The *third step* is to establish the amount of time to be given each category of school. The large schools will require more teacher time than the small schools if the student-teacher ratio is to be kept constant. Assuming that beginning classes are offered in the fifth grade and advanced classes in the sixth grade and that every student is to have two 30-minute periods of instruction each week, the instrumental music offerings might be set up like this:

The small school—4 hours of instructional time

First-year winds	Two 30-minute classes
First-year strings	Two 30-minute classes
Second-year winds	One 30-minute class (and orchestra)
Second-year strings	One 30-minute class (and orchestra)
Second-year orchestra	One 30-minute session
Individual help	One 30-minute period

The medium-sized school—6 hours of instructional time

First-year woodwinds	Two 30-minute classes
First-year brasswinds	Two 30-minute classes
First-year percussion	Two 30-minute classes
First-year strings	Two 30-minute classes
Second-year woodwinds	One 30-minute class (and orchestra)
Second-year brasswinds	One 30-minute class (and orchestra)
Second-year strings	One 30-minute class (and orchestra)
Second-year orchestra	One 30-minute session

The large school—9½ hours of instructional time

First-year flutes	Two 30-minute classes
First-year clarinets	Two 30-minute classes
First-year cornets	Two 30-minute classes
First-year trombones	Two 30-minute classes
First-year percussion	Two 30-minute classes
First-year strings	Two 30-minute classes
Second-year flutes	One 30-minute class (and orchestra)
Second-year clarinets	One 30-minute class (and orchestra)
Second-year cornets	One 30-minute class (and orchestra)
Second-year trombones	One 30-minute class (and orchestra)
Second-year percussion	One 30-minute class (and orchestra)
Second-year strings	One 30-minute class (and orchestra)
Second-year orchestra	One 30-minute session

It might be possible to reduce the teaching time in large schools by combining the classes for cornets and trombones or to expand it by adding a class for the double reeds or French horns. Other modifications might be made as readily.

The plan implies that each school is an entity, regardless of its size; it equalizes the pupil-teacher ratio among the schools; it reduces or eliminates the expensive 1:1 or 2:1 pupil-teacher ratio; and it assures each child an opportunity to learn music in the company of his classmates rather than alone.

SCHEDULING CLASSES
IN EACH SCHOOL

After the general plan for scheduling instrumental music in the elementary schools has been determined, teachers are assigned to buildings for specific days and hours. These assignments are usually made by the coordinator or supervisor in consultation with the several principals. From this point, all scheduling is usually the responsibility of the individual teacher, who must work closely with the principals of the schools in which he teaches. The teacher must consider the total program of each school as well as his own classes in order to avoid conflicts. He should be particularly careful to avoid conflicts with other teachers of special subjects who serve several buildings or can meet their students only once or twice weekly.

Scheduling should not begin until all necessary information has been gathered. The demonstration of instruments must have been followed by letters to parents and parental replies; the testing and selection of beginners must have been completed; and expected enrollments in second-year classes must have been identified. The teacher will need to know these facts about each child: name, grade level, and classroom teacher's name. By the time all the information has been assembled, usually the second or third week of school at best, the rest of the elementary school program will probably be in full swing. The instrumental music teacher must now work out the times of the specific classes with the least possible disturbance of activities already in progress.

The teacher must first obtain from the principal a schedule of all other special teachers that will identify their subjects and the classrooms in which they teach (with teachers' names and grade levels). Conflicts with these activities should be avoided or minimized. It might be possible, for example, to schedule a beginning flute class of girls at a time when the boys are scheduled for physical education and a class of trombones players (usually boys) while the girls are in the gymnasium. A number of such compromises may be made if all special teachers and the principal work together cordially.

With the special schedules and the list of instrumental students before him, the instrumental music teacher can work out the details of his schedule—a job that may take three or four days to complete. After the schedule has been approved by the principal and amended, if necessary, it is duplicated for the information of all teachers concerned. The schedule might appear as in the form on page 36.

Each classroom teacher should receive two copies of the schedule—one for the bulletin board and one for the desk. The children will be reminded of their appointments by the bulletin board copy, and the teacher will use the desk copy in planning her work and checking attendance.

The instrumental music teacher will find his copy of the schedule invaluable. If a student is absent from class, the schedule will indicate what room he should have come from and make it possible to send for him. The addition of students' telephone numbers to the instrumental music teacher's copy will facilitate calls to parents to discuss problems.

THE ROLE OF
THE CLASSROOM TEACHER

One of the most frequent complaints about instrumental music in elementary schools concerns the removal of children from the regular classroom routine. The many additions to the elementary school curriculum of the last few decades have

JONESVILLE ELEMENTARY SCHOOL

Instrumental Music Schedule

TIME	ROOM	TEACHER	MONDAY	THURSDAY
8:30	Aud.	Mr. Smith	Beg. Flute	Adv. Flute
	Music	Mr. Jones	Beg. Brass	Adv. Brass
9:00	Aud.	Mr. Smith	Beg. String	Adv. String
	Music	Mr. Jones	Beg. Clarinet	Adv. Clarinet
9:30	Aud.	Mr. Smith	Adv. Orch.	Beg. Orch.
	Music	Mr. Jones	Beg. Perc.	Adv. Perc.

Beg. Flute		Beg. Clarinet		Adv. Clarinet	
Sara Aris	R*	Bill Casto	N	Alma Alter	Ri
Albert Brown	N	Roger Hilbert	N	Bonnie Atkins	B
Shirley Cobb	N	Jack Leavy	E	Denny Davis	B
Dick Farris	E	Pete Ness	R	Fred Fauri	F
Linda Howard	R	Bicky Patner	R	Ora Hopkins	Es
Sally Mayo	S	Sue Rath	S	Susan Lea	F
		Tom Rizner	S	Bill Roach	B

Fifth-Grade Rooms		Sixth-Grade Rooms	
101	Miss Evans	202	Mr. Brown
103	Mrs. Nelson	204	Miss Falk
105	Mrs. Ransom	206	Mrs. Estes
107	Mr. Stark	208	Mr. Ritter

*The initials are those of the last names of the teachers.

intensified the problem. Interferences of any kind make the classroom teacher's job more difficult. It is only natural, then, that the classroom teacher asks, "What do I do with the rest of my class when so many students have gone to instrumental music?" or "How can I teach my classes with people coming and going all the time?" There are no easy answers.

The classroom teacher's difficulties with instrumental music can be reduced by an elementary school principal who believes in instrumental music and is sympathetic toward its aims. His attitude will influence the attitudes of his teachers and help establish an atmosphere in which the interruptions will be accepted more cheerfully because the reasons for them are understood. The principal may encourage his teachers to vary their classroom schedules to accommodate instrumental music students.

Classroom teachers who are enthusiastic about instrumental music will usually be willing to arrange their schedules so that instrumental music students need not miss the same subject each week. Or they will schedule subjects in which the missing students are particularly strong during instrumental music time. Instead of scheduling arithmetic, say, at ten o'clock every day, a sympathetic classroom teacher might schedule it at nine o'clock one day, eleven o'clock the next, and in mid-afternoon on another. Many classroom teachers like to rearrange their schedules a bit because they find the variety stimulating. Some school systems, however, forbid any departure from established room schedules. In these cases, the instrumental music schedule might be rotated.

When liaison is good between the instrumental music teacher and the classroom teacher, the classroom teacher will help to see that every child is regular in class attendance, that instruments are taken home regularly, and that children use their learning in other classroom activities. The cooperative teacher will also help by informing the instrumental music teacher of the problems of his students.

TEACHING TEAMS
IN INSTRUMENTAL MUSIC

When more than one instrumental music teacher is available in a school district, teaching teams are often used.[3] The thought behind this kind of assignment is simple—if one man needs eight hours to teach the students, two can do it in four hours, and four can get it done in just two hours! There are other implications that must be considered, however.

The teaching team plan offers certain advantages. Less school time is required and each teacher can work in his specialized area (woodwinds, brasswinds, or strings). While more students are absent from classrooms at any one time, the total disruption of classroom routine is reduced. However, the plan requires more teaching stations, uses more time in travel between schools, tends to create insecurity and loss of contact for teachers who have no "home base," makes it more difficult to co-ordinate teaching methods, and, sometimes, brings different teachers to the children in successive years.

[3] The term "teaching team" has been used for want of a better term. Such a team would be assigned to a building as a unit, conduct many of its affairs as a unit, but it would not organize the instruction of students nor attend classes as a teaching-team in academic courses would do.

When a teaching team is used, one member of the team should function as its head. His responsibilities would include organizing the demonstration, testing and selecting students, devising the schedule, conducting the band or orchestra, and negotiating with the principal. As the team moves from school to school, each member of the group should assume the headship for his share of the schools served.

If team assignments are not feasible, a single teacher will meet all instrumental music classes in any one school. This plan requires more school time but takes fewer students from any one classroom at any one time. The teacher may become better acquainted with students and parents because he works with them for two years. Only one teaching station is needed, and travel time is reduced to a minimum. The constancy of teaching methods is enhanced. However, the teacher must be competent on all the instruments he is to teach.

STARTING BEGINNERS
IN THE SUMMER

Some schools have found it advantageous to start instruction on musical instruments during a six-week or eight-week summer session. Enrollment is usually limited to students who have just completed the fourth grade. Sometimes the summer program is exclusively devoted to exploratory classes or to classes in pre-band instruments. With summer instruction available, selections of new students can be made well before the opening of the school year.

However, many children will attend summer classes irregularly if at all because of family vacation plans. Some students are placed in the difficult position of having to choose between instrumental music and summer camp. Therefore, beginning classes should be offered during the school year as well as during the summer.

Under no circumstances should students with summer experience be scheduled with new beginners in the fall, nor should first-year students be scheduled with second-year students. This kind of scheduling only leads to boredom and disenchantment for the advanced students who are held back by the ineptness of the inexperienced. And the younger students are frustrated and discouraged when they cannot keep up with their older classmates.

In some schools, when financial support has been reduced or withdrawn from the elementary school instrumental music program, after-school and Saturday classes have augmented summer instruction, often at additional cost to the students. While such scheduling might be defended as enabling the continuance of an established secondary school band or orchestra, it is evidence that the school's administrators and constituents have lost sight of the primary goals of instrumental music instruction.

SCHEDULING
ALL-CITY GROUPS

All-city bands and orchestras can be rich and rewarding experiences for students and teachers if the music is of high caliber and the activity is very well organized. Many school systems provide these groups because the bands and orchestras of individual elementary schools often lack complete instrumentation. All-city groups provide children with a great deal more musical stimulation than can the orchestras of individual schools.

All-city groups are extracurricular and should be scheduled after school or on Saturdays. In organizing an all-city band or orchestra, permission of the administration must be secured first. The better and more advanced students should then be selected by audition or by teachers' recommendations so that the activity becomes a reward for excellence. Parents should be notified by letter of the dates, times, places, and duration of rehearsals, and, if possible, the dates of performance. Transportation should be provided by parents.

6

The First
Few Lessons

Very little that the instrumental music teacher does has more importance than the first lessons he gives to a class of beginners. During the early days, when his students' interest and curiosity are highest, the teacher sets the tone for their entire musical careers. So crucial are these days that some instrumental music teachers rearrange their schedules so that the beginning classes receive more than their usual time allotment. Even when this cannot be done, the finest instrumental music teachers take great care that their other responsibilities do not interfere with a good start for the recruits.

THE IMPORTANCE
OF A GOOD START

Playing a musical instrument is not really difficult. What makes it seem difficult is the effort required to overcome normal human inertia plus poor habits. Human inertia remains essentially a problem for the individual, but poor habits result from inadequate teaching and can therefore be prevented by improvement in teaching techniques.

As the child approaches his instrumental music class for the first time he is in a particularly favorable psychological condition. The prospect of learning to play an instrument is an exciting one. At his first lesson he is ready to believe anything his teacher says, do anything his teacher suggests. The teacher must therefore be sure that he asks of the child only responses that will be correct at the moment and *correct as long as the student continues to play*. The child will perform as he has been taught to perform, read as he has been taught to read, behave as he has been taught to behave. During the first few lessons, he sets up standards against which he will measure himself (and be measured by others) in:

Class conduct	Articulation	Playing by ear
Instrument care	Breathing	Thinking
Beating time	Fingering	Responding
Tone	Hearing	Cooperating
Posture	Playing in tune	Enjoying

Because he is experiencing all these for the first time in his life—at least as related to instrumental music—he has no bad habits to break. Hopefully, the teacher will build nothing but good habits!

THE FIRST CLASS MEETING

Instrumental music teachers are busy people with multiple responsibilities in several schools. What is suggested below may not be feasible for all, but the closer the teacher of beginners can approach these standards the more effective will be his first meeting with a new class.

When the students first enter the room, the teacher will greet them warmly—but not too warmly. Until he knows his students well, he might better remain a step or two away in friendliness; yet he must not dampen their enthusiasm by being overly harsh or officious.

Chairs will be in place as the teacher wishes his class to be seated. Music stands will not be needed because there will be no reading of music for several lessons. As the students come in they may be directed to their assigned seats by the use of placards bearing their names. This little extra detail will help create an atmosphere for work and attention.

If students bring their own instruments, they should be told to put the cases on the floor next to their chairs and to leave the cases closed until the time comes to open them. If the instruments are provided by the school, the teacher will have placed each instrument beside its proper chair (after having checked its condition and the presence of accessories).

It should take only a moment for students to find their places and come to order. The teacher introduces himself, writing his name on the chalkboard to help impress it upon the children. He may then ask each child to introduce himself. If he notates his schedule sheet or class roll with pronunciation cues, he will find that he can henceforth pronounce every name in the class correctly.

This is not the time for speech-making, so the teacher will begin by teaching the children how to open the instrument cases. This must be done with great care, for the children have no way of knowing which is the top or the bottom of the case or how the locks and clasps operate. In any class, the first step must be to insure that the case is right side up and to teach the children how to know this. A few cases are symmetrical; identification of the top half by manufacturer's mark or some other sign must be taught. As this is being done, the teacher's remarks will be explanatory and admonitory. This is his first chance to teach the children to respect their instruments. He can overdo by lecturing, of course, but he must impress the students with the need for care.

Young students in new situations are easily confused; they may not even be sure about "right" and "left." The teacher will need to demonstrate very carefully, particularly if he is facing the class. If he can arrange to do some of the demonstration with his back partially turned to the class, his movements will be easier for the children to imitate.

The next step will depend upon how the teacher intends to approach tone production. If he wishes to start the students with the mouthpiece alone, he will identify the mouthpiece by description and demonstration, asking the students to take this part out of the case without disturbing anything else. If he wishes to spend the first class teaching assembly of the instrument, he will identify by name and demonstration each of the parts in the order that they are to be taken from the case.

The choice of starting with the mouthpiece alone or with the entire instrument will depend upon two principal factors: Are the students to be taught embouchure formation before anything else, and are they to take their instruments home between classes? Most successful instructors probably devote the first lesson to embouchure formation without assembling the instrument so that the attention of the children is riveted on the importance of good embouchure. However, if the instruments are to be taken home between lessons the correct method of assembly must be taught because the children will be sure to try to put them together as soon as they can. If they do not know what they are doing, they will be very likely to cause damage that will necessitate doing without instruments, and hence learning less than they should, at later lessons.

If it is at all possible, the instructor should insist that all instruments be kept at school until he is satisfied that the children can play and handle them without supervision. Keeping the instruments at school makes it possible to capitalize on interest and curiosity. The children have only one or two short periods with their new instruments every week. They can hardly wait for the instrumental music class to begin. And during the class period they work at great intensity. If the instructor can keep the instruments at school, he can also prevent the students from learning the bad habits sure to develop when children experiment without understanding.

The teacher should inform parents, in the letter announcing the first meeting of the class, that instruments are not to be taken home and why this procedure is important. He should also establish the standards that his students must meet before they may take the instruments away from the school. These criteria might include satisfactory embouchure and tone, skill in handling the instrument, ability to play two or three songs by rote or memory, and firmly established habits of beating time and holding the instrument. The teacher must realize that once instruments are taken home between classes he has lost a large part of his control over the development of his students and has also lost the great advantage provided by their curiosity.

Throughout the first lessons, the wise teacher will be sure that he proceeds in readily conquerable steps. He must never go so rapidly that his students become confused; nor must he go so slowly that they become bored. He must be confident that every lesson results in steady progress toward the goals he has set and that every lesson is a meaningful and exciting experience that will foster a desire to learn more and more about music and the instruments. He must be sure that no lesson is only half-taught. Between class meetings the students practice, or at least think about what they have learned. If they have learned incorrectly, they can only practice and think incorrectly. Incorrect learnings become habitual, and the effort required to break these early bad habits is often so great that student and teacher become disenchanted.

If possible, the first lesson should conclude with a musical experience no matter how rudimentary. In a brass class it should be fairly easy to produce a tone on the mouthpiece or the instrument, to articulate by rote, and to sustain tones. In a woodwind class or a mixed class this may not be feasible since there are more problems of instrument assembly. If nothing else can be done, the first practice in beating time might be given.

THE NEXT FEW CLASSES

From now on, as students come into the room, they are expected to do so in an orderly, quiet manner—neither talking nor playing until permission has been granted. They should take the places assigned to them, putting the instrument cases beside the chairs until told to open the cases. Every sound that is made in the instrumental music classroom should be a sound in response to a musical demand and a sound that is under control.

The first few classes should introduce embouchure formation, tone production, breathing, fingering, counting, imitating rhythms played or sung by the teacher, posture, and acceptable behavior. The musical material should be learned by rote; the children have quite enough challenges without adding the mysteries of staff notation. Too much emphasis on notation in the first few weeks means that there cannot be enough time for adequate preparation of embouchure, tone production, and ear training.

Once the class has begun to produce an adequate tone, the teacher should introduce other pitches and their fingerings so that little melodies may be played. This process can be continued for some time without harm since, while it is going on, the children are learning a great deal about music, about handling the instruments, and about making music. They are also learning to use their ears. Notation study at this time often encourages the development of notation-to-muscle conditioned responses without the intervention of the ear. This can be disastrous when key signatures and accidentals are added to the problems of performance and, in its most severe manifestations, may lead to completely unmusical performances. The child who has learned to *hear* that the melody or the harmony demand a note fingered with the first finger alone (as on the clarinet, for example) is much closer to being a musician than the child who knows that the first finger is right only because the note is on the first space of the staff and that there is an odd-looking sign on the top staff line.

As the students progress, they accumulate a repertoire of songs that they enjoy playing for themselves and for their parents. These rote songs may be transposed or played with altered rhythms or treated in a number of ways to increase the children's skills. There comes a time when this is no longer enough; in order to learn more songs the students need to learn to read music. Now the instructor issues books and begins the first lessons on notation. The first reading lessons will be based on melodic and rhythmic patterns the children have already learned by rote.

MAKING ASSIGNMENTS

Every lesson should conclude with the making of an assignment for the next class meeting and the intervening days. The assignment should be realistic, asking of the children only what they can reasonably be expected to accomplish. It should be very carefully explained. A class should never be dismissed with the direction to "Learn the next five exercises" if there is the slightest chance that some part of those exercises calls for skills or knowledge the children have not acquired.

When the students are working from books, the assignment will be more meaningful if it can be noted in the books by the teacher. This may be done quickly while instruments are being put away. A simple comment or a circle drawn around the exercise numbers will usually suffice and will let the child and his parents know exactly what is expected. Since the teacher will have several classes and will probably not be able to keep all of them moving at the same pace, he should keep a record of assignments in a notebook or a classroom teacher's plan book.

7

Basic Principles
of Class Instruction
in Instrumental Music

Since its inception in the early decades of the twentieth century the teaching of instrumental music in the public schools has been influenced in its methodology by divergent forces and philosophies. On the one hand, the tradition of the instrumental music class derived in part from the tradition of the military band with its emphasis on discipline and routinized learning. On the other, instrumental music teaching had traditionally been the province of the private studio. When instrumental music became part of the school curriculum it came under the influence of educators and musicians whose philosophies had been derived from the thinking of Pestalozzi, Mason, Dewey, Farnsworth, and Earhart. To these influences was added that of the need to develop playing bands in the shortest possible time.

Those instrumental programs that have been most successful in attaining great heights of artistry while at the same time serving the total student population seem to have been founded on an empirical eclecticism; actual experience has led to the acceptance of portions of each of the philosophies and traditions and combined them into a pragmatic philosophy that includes the following premises:

A. The purpose of music instruction in the schools is to enable students to develop a love and understanding of music.

B. Instrumental music is but one of the ways by which this may be accomplished. For almost all students it is a way of enlarging experience; for some students it is the way of choice.

C. Establishment of correct performance and behavioral habits is a *means* of reaching the goals of music instruction, not the goal itself.

D. Therefore, all instruction in instrumental music must be organized in such a way that the ultimate goals—development of love and understanding of music—are constantly kept in mind.

In consideration of these statements and of the democratic character of American elementary schools, the beginning instrumental music class should be organized and conducted on the basis of principles that may be said to depend upon these basic premises.

PRINCIPLE I

Underlying all instruction, in music as well as in other subjects, is the principle that learning is often most effective when *experience precedes theory*, or, in Pestalozzian terms, the thing before the sign. Progressing from the known to the unknown, the learner remakes his experience. Having learned, he has changed to the extent that his understanding of his experiences has been altered.

The implications of this principle are of vital importance. Assume that a child comes to his first cornet lesson and that the terms of the principle are reversed—theory about the cornet is to precede experience with the cornet. The teacher might speak of the acoustics of the cornet, of its fascinating history, of the musculature of the face, of scales and chords and signatures. Will the child learn to play the cornet in this lesson? Decidedly not. He will learn something, of course—those facts that are within the range of his experience and understanding. But the bare array of facts does not produce a change in the child nor does it really help him toward his goal. How, then, should the first cornet lesson be organized in accordance with Principle I?

Instead of talking about the cornet, the instructor will demonstrate it, playing just a few tones. He will ask the child to observe the formation of his lips. As the child attempts to emulate his teacher, the vicarious experiences of observation lead to real experiences that become increasingly successful. When the child can produce his first real tone on the instrument, he has changed—he will never be quite the same. His unsuccessful attempts lead to thoughtful change and eventual correction.

His successful attempts are reinforcements of experience that lead to competence.

In the teaching of rhythms, the same principle applies. Instead of dividing pies into fractions (often before the child knows what fractions are), the child keeps time by walking. A step is a beat or a count. One can do two things in one step, or take two steps to do something. Eighth notes and half notes become meaningful when they are presented as signs for something the child already knows.

Principle I does not imply that all instruction must proceed at a slow pace. Nor does it imply that the inspiration of curiosity be denied. Children often want to know more than their experience permits them to understand *fully*. Their questions and experiments should be welcomed and responded to in ways that are immediately meaningful and permanently useful.

PRINCIPLE II

Obviously, not all students in any class have had the same experiences, nor have they all been equally successful in understanding their experiences. Therefore, the teacher must organize instruction in such a way as to proceed *from the known to the unknown*. When children have not had the experiences needed for understanding, the teacher must supply those experiences, relating them to already-understood experiences.

Students enter classes with insufficient foundation even in the very best of situations. Inequalities of educational opportunity, unequal strengths of teachers, and the diversity of children's interests and abilities lead to wide variations in the experiences children bring to their first music class. The successful teacher will therefore discover as much as he can about his students and institute remedial or review activities for those whose backgrounds have been deficient. He will also remember to review constantly, knowing that students rapidly forget unused skills and information.

Principle II has other implications for the instrumental music class. Suppose a class is being challenged by a new key signature. The teacher might talk about the key, the placement of the sign on the staff, and tell the student how to finger the new note (violating Principle I as he does so). Preferably, the teacher will ask the children to seek out what is new by observing the staff or hearing the teacher play. Then, when the students play, their own ears tell them what is different and many will discover for themselves what must be done to make the music sound right.

Another application of Principle II uses a mirror, one of the finest of teaching aids. Young students have no way of knowing what to do with their lip muscles in order to form an embouchure. Their attempts at imitating the teacher's grimaces are often so far wide of the mark as to be ludicrous. If teacher and child can look together at the mirror as the teacher shapes his embouchure, the child will quickly learn to approximate the right formation. Finger positions are also much better exemplified if teacher and student are side by side, both looking at the same effect.

PRINCIPLE III

The learning process proceeds most effectively when it is organized in such a way that the specific is related to the general and the general to the specific—in other words, *from the whole to the parts and back again.* What constitutes an appropriate "whole" will vary. Sometimes an appropriate "whole" will be the production of a single tone; at others it will be a complete piece of music. The proper balancing of "wholes" and "parts" requires careful thought.

Principle III is violated when an instructor becomes so insistent on minute details that the total musical effect is lost. It is violated when a teacher spends an entire class period on drill without providing an opportunity to play a piece of music straight through without a stop—as music must be played. But it is also violated when he fails to point out and work on the details that must be mastered in order to make the whole piece sound good.

PRINCIPLE IV

Throughout the educational process, the teacher must realize that the important activity in the classroom is not teaching but learning, and that *learning depends upon the desire to learn.* Going to school may be made compulsory, but learning—that is, the active participation of the student in the process of being educated and thereby changed—is an individual and voluntary activity. The child may respond to the demands of his teacher by memorizing data or acting in unexceptional ways, but this is not necessarily to say that he is learning.

The child learns because he does not know the answers and wants to know them. The teacher must therefore set before the child tasks that are meaningful to the child at the moment. The child lives in the present; his is a world of "here and now," rather than the teacher's world of "sometime, somewhere in the future." The implications for instrumental beginning classes will affect the choice of materials, the methods of presentation, and the general management of the classroom situation.

For the child it is far more important to play today's melodies to his own satisfaction, and, perhaps, to his teacher's, than it is to play today's exercises because they will make it easier for him to play a sonata five years from now. The child finds more value in meeting the immediate challenges of his classmates than some more difficult challenge to be faced in an unknown situation far in the future. The skilled teacher will capitalize on the child's need for immediate response by organizing the instruction so as to guarantee continuing progress toward those goals that only the teacher can see while at the same time satisfying the child's need for immediate success.

PRINCIPLE V

If learning depends on wanting to learn, then *teaching is the art of making students want to learn.* In the beginning instrumental music class, then, teaching is *not* conducting, *not* lecturing, *not* judging. Teaching *is* motivating, explaining, demonstrating, encouraging, suggesting, organizing, and evaluating.

The skillful teacher of the beginning class will know what his pupils need to know and will create a situation so hospitable to learning that the students will be impatient for the opportunity to learn. The teacher will remember that the greatest pleasures a child can have are often those of discovery. He will encourage his pupils to search for questions implicit in every assignment and help them find the answers. He will not do all the work for them, defining the problem and telling them the solution. Many, if not all, of the problems encountered by young musicians in a well-organized class are within their abilities to solve; they should be permitted to seek their own solutions. When difficulties arise, or when the class cannot discover the problem, the teacher recalls Principles I, II, and III and organizes the instruction accordingly.

8

Effective
Classroom
Control

Every meeting of the instrumental music class must be a period devoted to the work at hand and should be completed with some evident progress toward the goals of instruction. The teacher is responsible for setting the tone of the class and creating an atmosphere in which the desired learnings may take place. His success will be determined in large part by the amount of control he exercises over the learning situation, including the physical characteristics of the classroom.

CLASSROOM EQUIPMENT

It is essential that all equipment be ready for use at the beginning of the class period. Chairs and stands should be in place so that no instructional time need be sacrificed for housekeeping chores. Whenever possible the equipment should be put in place by students for whom the activity becomes part of their training as responsible school citizens.

In some teaching situations, instrumental music classes are taught in rooms used for other purposes during part of the school day and vacated just before the instrumental music class is to begin. In these cases, it is suggested that the instructor establish a careful routine, utilizing his students in the most effective way. If the class is small, little loss of teach-time will result and confusion can be kept to a minimum. If the class is large, however, the planning must be done very carefully and the established rules strictly observed. Since students in the elementary schools are apt to be careless in handling chairs and stands, it may be advisable to insist that instruments be left in cases until all, or nearly all, students are settled so that instruments will not be damaged.

The proper arrangement of chairs and stands will depend in part on the physical facilities available and on the size of the class. However, a few general rules apply. The beginning class is *not* a band. Chairs and stands need not be arranged in semicircles about a podium; rather, the students should be seated in such a way that the teacher may circulate freely among them, offering suggestions and correcting errors. The teacher will find this easiest if chairs are arranged in parallel rows.

A podium is almost useless with a class of beginners and, in fact, may be detrimental to instruction since it tends to become a fixed spot for the teacher. The most effective teacher will move about the room constantly, listening to individuals as much as he listens to the sound of the whole group. Removing himself from a central point, he enables his students to become independent of him in maintaining steady tempos, subdividing beats, and checking their own progress.

After the first lesson, instrument cases should be placed under the chairs so that the aisles will be clear at all times. Players of the larger instruments should leave their cases around the outside walls of the room or in some other spot where they will not interfere with the movement of the teacher and students.

Ideally, every room for instrumental music instruction should have instrument storage space. Children should be taught, from the first class meeting, to store instruments in the proper places and to keep the storage area free of other materials. When instruments must be kept in areas remote from the instrumental music room or in the regular classrooms, the instructor should make every effort to insure that the instruments are properly taken care of during the hours that class is not in session.

A chalkboard is essential, for it enables every student in the class to observe a single item visually, and let the instructor see that they are doing it. When explanations are made as students look at their own books, the instructor has no way of knowing whether all his students are even on the right page. If errors then occur the cooperative attitude of the class is destroyed—or, at least, the forward progress is slowed.

Small mirrors that can be placed on the music stands will be very valuable in demonstrating embouchure formation at the beginning of the term. The mirrors should be about the size of the ordinary beginning class method book.

BEGINNING THE CLASS PERIOD

Once the class is in place, the teacher indicates that instruments are to be taken from the cases and assembled. During this period, the teacher should move about the room observing the condition of instruments and the care taken in assembling them. Many correct habits can be reinforced and bad habits eliminated if the teacher uses this part of the class period for instruction.

When all is ready, the teacher announces the first activity of the period and class instruction begins. The attention of the class may be obtained by some established signal—perhaps the presence of the teacher at a point in front of the class, a nod of the head, or simply an announcement that the class will begin with a certain activity. The teacher should avoid trying to talk over the conversation of the class or the noise of assembly. Shouting over class noises is rarely successful, since it tends to become more and more necessary as it is used.

If the teacher can be consistent, he will be able to be friendly to his students without any sacrifice in discipline. And if he can establish desirable procedures at the first meetings of the class, he will save himself and his students a great deal of unpleasantness.

All the above will be accomplished, by a well-trained class, in much less time than it takes to read about it. Instructional time will be saved, valuable disciplinary lessons will be learned, and students and teacher will be able to start the class period with a cordial relationship.

Occasionally, a teacher falls into the habit of using the period between classes to absent himself from the classroom. If he enters the room after his students and is displeased with their behavior, he should realize that the fault is his. Elementary school children are so volatile that a momentary lapse in supervision may be enough to disrupt completely the established routines, and precious instructional time may be lost in restoring normalcy.

THE WORK AT HAND

The activities for any class period should be carefully planned to provide for class and individual progress, evaluation, individual differences, review of old material, and assignment of new material. The following is a discussion of methods that will help each class meeting to be productive.

One of the surest means of guaranteeing a good learning situation is to *use the period for the work at hand.* Good order depends to a great extent upon keeping all the students busy at appropriate tasks every minute of the period. In the beginning instrumental music class, with its myriad individual problems with children, instruments, and music, the task is not as easy as it is in some other kinds of instruction. However, if the teacher will bear in mind all the things he is trying to teach, he can find ways of occupying the attention of every student at all times.

First, of course, he must remember that the beginning instrument class is a place for students to learn to play and that they learn to play *by playing.* He will talk as little as possible and try to speak only of those matters that have immediate application. The lecture method, so prevalent on college and university campuses, is perhaps one of the poorest ways of imparting non-factual information. In the elementary school, it often fails completely because the students have not yet acquired a sufficient fund of knowledge and experience to make a lecture vivid; therefore, demonstration and trials are much more likely to produce results in the beginning class. Even errors and their correction are preferable to long lectures on how to avoid making mistakes.

The beginning class will be most successful if all the students can be working with music as much of the period as possible. The admonition to "keep them playing" is particularly appropriate. As the students play assigned exercises, the instructor listens for faults, corrects individual deficiencies, and then, quickly and concisely, tells the class what is needed for better performance, or he leads the students to make the appropriate suggestions. The shorter the time span between the error and its correction, the more effective the instruction will be. When repetitions are needed, the reasons should be given. No class should be asked to repeat an exercise unless it has been told *why* to repeat and *what* to do to make further repetitions unnecessary. This admonition applies to drill material as well. It is sometimes necessary to isolate a problem and to work on it a dozen or more times. If the students can be made to understand that the drill is needed in order to make a correct response habitual, they will work on it with enthusiasm. If, on the other hand, they are repeating without any apparent reason, members of the group will let their attention wander, retard the progress of the group, and make the drill less valuable.

The instructor listens for good points as well as for errors, and then shows his appreciation of improvement frequently. Since students are eager to do the right thing, the instructor should capitalize on their eagerness by acknowledging successes.

REST PERIODS THAT WORK

Because the students in a begin-
ning class have not yet developed sufficient muscular strength to play
for long periods at a time, the instructor must provide frequent moments
of rest. However, these moments are for the relaxation of lip muscles,
not for the cessation of attention to the problems at hand. Several devices will be found useful for the most efficient use of lip-resting periods.
One is to have the resting members of the class provide some kind of
accompaniment for those who are still playing. They can beat time (perhaps with the traditional conductor's gestures), count aloud, name the
notes, sing, or listen and make constructive suggestions. Each of these
activities keeps the attention of the resting students on the musical material and provides practice in skills they need to acquire for their own
benefit. The resting students may also be asked to finger the exercises
silently.

Another device, useful for providing rest time and also for the evaluation of student progress, is the relay solo. An exercise is first played
through by the entire class. Then each member in turn plays two or four
measures. The resting students follow their parts, fingering the notes
and counting aloud. Sometimes the order of performance should be evident (from one person to his neighbor); at other times the order should
be random (the teacher calling for the next player a beat or two before
his turn). When this is done, no allowances should be made for the correction of errors. Each student is to complete his assigned measures on
time, and his successor should start at the right place on the right beat,
no matter what disasters have occurred.

This technique can be used to provide for individual recitation and
competition as is done in classes at the National Music Camp.[1]

A. After the class has played a piece once or twice, the teacher points to the
pupil in the back seat of Row One and says, "Next." Whereupon that pupil
plays the piece (or the first phrase) alone while the other pupils listen critically.

B. If the pupil plays the piece correctly the other pupils repeat (without
losing a beat) as a sign of approval. If played correctly (in the judgment of
the class), the next pupil (the one in front of the first) tries, while the class
listens. If played incorrectly the class does not repeat and the next pupil tries.
If this pupil plays correctly, and the class repeats in approval, the second player
changes seats with the one who failed. This routine shifts the better players to
the back seats and the weaker players to the front seats where they may
receive more help from the teacher without disrupting the progress of the class.

[1] Joseph E. Maddy, "Fourteen Steps to Musicianship" (Interlochen, Michigan:
Interlochen Press), p. 17.

Still another device is the surprise solo (or duet, trio, or quartet). The class plays the exercise once. Then, when it is repeated, the instructor suddenly announces, "First row only," or "Cornets only," or "Just Mary Jane and Jeannette." He may then proceed with other combinations at will.

Still another use of rest periods is to conduct a "Name-the-Note-I-Finger Contest." The instructor or a student stands before the class and, holding the instrument high so that all may see, places the fingers properly for one of the notes all have learned. The students respond by calling out the note name or by identifying by line or space the location of the note on the staff.

Since ear-training is a part of the program of the beginning instrumental music class, another use of rest periods is to let students take turns playing "mystery measures." One student begins, playing a passage chosen from any exercise on the page. His classmates try to locate the measures before he has finished the passage. The first person to identify the spot plays the next set of "mystery measures." Another ear-training exercise that children enjoy is to have the instructor, facing away from the students or standing behind them, play a note all have learned and to ask individuals to repeat that tone. A point of reference should always be established—"This is C; now what is *this* note?"

Some lip-resting periods will be taken up by the teacher in the presentation of new problems and solutions, reviews of procedures, and other matters essential to the progress of the class. This type of rest period is most useful when it is short, well-organized, and immediately applicable.

CORRECTING PERFORMANCE AND BEHAVIORAL ERRORS

No matter how skillful the teacher and how brilliant the class, errors will occur. The fine teacher will treat musical and behavioral errors as a fine doctor treats physiological and psychological ailments—patiently, clinically, and with attention to the most serious problems first. Patience is essential. Young students rarely make errors on purpose. Their errors are usually honest mistakes, caused by lack of experience, the awkwardness of unfamiliar instruments and positions, the inherent mysteries of notation, or (tragically often) the failure of the instructor to make his meaning clear. When mistakes occur, the wise instructor simply suggests how the errors may be corrected, or he may ask the student to analyze the problem and help the learner search for the correct response. The wise teacher will not lose his sense of humor, nor will he treat an error as a challenge to his own "mighty" position.

Approaching the error clinically, the teacher attempts first to find the reason for it (accident, improper or misunderstood instruction, lack of attention, or faulty instrument). He then takes whatever corrective measures are required. If he is careful, he never embarrasses a student by chastizing him at length for a little slip, nor does he encourage carelessness by ignoring habitual gross mistakes.

Some children will be so upset by their errors that no comment from the teacher is needed. Some will be disturbed and seek guidance to prevent repetition of the errors. Others will have been made so fearful of mistakes and corrective techniques that they have become unreachable, and a few will actually welcome the errors they make because they get the attention they so sorely need. A well-organized class, with a conscientious, patient, clinical, friendly teacher, will develop a healthy attitude toward errors. Students will realize that perfection is greatly to be desired but extremely difficult to attain. They will learn to anticipate possible errors and search out ways to avoid them. They will look upon their teacher as one who can help them reach their goals rather than as a stern, avenging tyrant.

Whatever the teacher does in the elimination of errors, he should do in a calm, businesslike manner. The temper tantrums that have added spice to the legends about famous musicians have no place in the beginning class, or, indeed, any place in public school music. True, students and classes occasionally need to be "brought into line." Scolding sometimes helps; but displays of temper never do anything but weaken the respect of the students for their teacher. Actually, too frequent scolding can often be harmful. Some students are talked to and scolded so much that they soon learn to let unpleasant words pass over them, and, sometimes, students find temper tantrums so entertaining that they think up ways to provoke them.

In correcting errors or modifying classroom behavior, the teacher must use appropriate standards, realistic in terms of the specific situation. It is useless to expect the same performance or the same behavior of youngsters at the beginning of a course of instruction as will prevail after competence has been achieved. The teacher of a young class will sometimes have to overlook undesirable things. He will have to accept poor tones, bad intonation, insecure rhythms, sloppy posture, *but only if they are not as poor as they have been before.* No one can expect a beginner to sound as good or to understand as well as an advanced player. All that can be expected is reasonably steady progress from inefficiency to efficiency, from insecurity to confidence, from raucous noise to beautiful tone.

THE TEACHER MUST KNOW
HIS STUDENTS

One of the surest ways of guaranteeing the attention of a class and of preventing behavioral errors is for the teacher to be obviously and sincerely interested in what every child is doing at all times. The teacher must learn to attend to every student, as an individual, while conducting the activities of the whole group. He must learn to watch one student solve a fingering problem, listen to another student's tone, and hear the performance of the whole class—all at the same instant. He can then stop the little errors of performance and behavior before they become habitual. The better he knows his students as individuals, the easier his task will be.

The teacher *should know his students* well enough to be able to correct their individual errors in suitable ways or to share their joys when they make little successes. He should know their idiosyncrasies, their individual performance problems, their psychological states, and their physical characteristics.

The successful teacher *respects his students.* He learns their names quickly, pronounces and spells them correctly. He respects the child's name and his body, the two things that the child has as distinctively his own. He respects the name by using it as the child uses it and by avoiding unpleasant nicknames. He respects the child's body by refraining from poking fingers to the correct keys, punching the abdomen to encourage correct breathing, touching the corners of the mouth to help form the embouchure. In short, an effective teacher finds ways to teach that do not require touching the child in any way. When verbal descriptions and visual and aural demonstrations have failed, then—and only then—should the teacher ask the child if he may help. When he does so, he might be wise to use the tip of a pencil rather than his finger.

The successful teacher shows his respect for students in other ways. He cannot treat every student alike because students differ so greatly. But he can create a situation in which each student is able to achieve his maximum musical potential. The truly skilled teacher is friendly. He brings to each of his pupils an attitude of acceptance and demonstrates his willingness to help each according to his needs. He is informal rather than stiff because he knows that elementary school children react unfavorably to over-repression and that strict formalism can stifle their abilities to learn on their own and to help each other. He is businesslike because he is continually aware of his responsibility to organize and control the teaching-learning processes taking place in his classroom. He treats every student with equal degrees of fairness, impartiality, and consideration.

The skillful teacher *recognizes that success engenders success* and that all persons enjoy doing things in which they can succeed. The obvious corollary is that no one enjoys failing. The fine teacher, therefore, does all that he can to insure that his students will succeed. He assigns tasks that are within their present abilities and rewards them in proportion to the difficulty of the task. Even partial successes deserve some credit. The teacher who speaks to his students only of their faults creates resentments, fosters discouragement, accelerates the rate of drop-out, and builds for himself an emotional attitude that can only lead to physical or mental anguish. This is not to say that all tasks must be easy nor that easy successes are desirable; the tasks must be challenging but appropriate. The student must be shown the importance of the task and helped in solving its problems.

ENCOURAGING
CLASS PARTICIPATION

Frequently, the teacher of a beginning instrumental music class may enhance the learning atmosphere of his classroom by encouraging the students to assume some responsibility for planning the instruction. Children are often more aware of their immediate needs than the instructor can be and will request repetitions of material with which they feel insecure. They can also help the teacher and each other by expressing in their own language the topic under discussion. The instrumental music teacher should pattern his teaching procedures upon the practices of the finest elementary school teachers he can observe. The best teachers are likely to be those who subscribe to the thesis that, essentially, it is the learner who does the learning and that the teacher's role is to organize, coordinate, encourage, and clarify. Care must be taken, however, to see that every member of the class has an opportunity to express his views and that every statement of opinion be treated with the seriousness with which it is offered. No child should be made to feel rejected because his offering is inappropriate or erroneous.

INSISTENCE
ON FUNDAMENTALS

The teacher of the beginning instrumental class must be steadfast in his efforts to establish and maintain proper playing and behavioral patterns. Every meeting of the class should provide some opportunity for him to lead his students toward the final goals he has set for them. It is in the beginning classes that good bands and orchestras develop, for here the students are most likely to be receptive. They are interested in working hard at tasks that seem worthwhile and are eager to emulate the successful students who have preceded them. The instructor should capitalize on these traits, "selling" good performance habits, good posture, good behavior—building from the very first lessons those traditions which will lead to the success of his students and of the organizations they will join after they leave elementary school.

As the students progress through the first year of instruction, the notational and performance challenges they meet become more and more difficult. It is easy for them, and sometimes for their instructor, to spend so much time mastering a new problem that they forget the good habits they learned in the first weeks of class. The instructor will need to be constantly alert to any sloughing off of fundamentals. He will need to be patient, firm, and inventive, for he will find that teaching often means saying the same things over and over in many, many different ways.

WHEN DISCIPLINE LAPSES

When disciplinary infractions occur, as they will in even the best of classes, the skillful teacher will remain calm, dignified, and will quickly regain control of the situation. Any violation of established standards of behavior is a sign of some maladjustment and must be treated as such. If the misbehavior is the result of emotional problems of the student, emotionalism on the part of the instructor can only compound the problem. If possible, serious disciplinary problems should be treated by isolating the miscreant and postponing action until all parties are able to discuss the matter dispassionately.

However, most problems will not require such radical procedures. Usually a few words of reprimand or a glance at the offender will suffice, provided the teacher has established attitudes of fair play and mutual respect. In no case should the teacher be dishonest with his students. He should not threaten punishments that he cannot carry out, nor should he promise rewards he cannot deliver. If the teacher will be as clinical about disciplinary problems as he should be about performance problems, he will find that his classes can go for weeks without serious disturbances once the proper foundations have been laid.

Perhaps the best way for a teacher to improve the discipline of his class is to improve himself. He should strive to change his own personality for the better, to know his students better, to master his teaching material more thoroughly, and to know more and more about the instruments he is teaching his students to play. He should become increasingly aware of the potential pitfalls in the material he presents to his classes and be constantly on the alert to improve his teaching techniques.

CO-OPERATING WITH
OTHER TEACHERS

Instrumental music teachers often create difficulties for themselves by failing to realize the needs of teachers of other subjects or the demands of elementary school organization. Classes must start and end exactly on time, for the child in the elementary school has no place to go except to another classroom. If he is dismissed early, he can only disturb another class. The schedule established by the principal must be adhered to with the greatest of accuracy. The instrumental music teacher must be particularly careful to notify elementary school principals if he must be absent or late.

Because instrumental music classes are inherently noisy, students should never be permitted to play until the door of the room is closed; nor should students be permitted to play their instruments in the corridors of the building.

If the instrumental music teacher can establish friendly relations with the classroom teachers, the secretarial helpers, and the custodians, he will find his work lightened immeasurably. These people are as interested in the children as he is and often have access to information that will help him work more effectively. Classroom teachers can be particularly helpful because they are well aware of the learning capabilities and behavioral characteristics of every one of their students.

9

Posture
and Breathing

Certain factors of performance on wind instruments are basic to all
others. Posture and breathing are essential elements of fine playing
and should be reviewed constantly. Each of these factors is so fundamental that the neglect of either puts the student in the position of
fighting himself and his instrument in order to play at all. If these
factors have been thoroughly mastered, as they have been by all true
artists, playing an instrument becomes easy.

POSTURE:
SITTING AND STANDING

Singers and wind instrument
players function at their best when they are able to support their tones
with adequate supplies of air and when their bodies are as free of tensions
as possible. For these reasons, fine performers hold the upper part of the
body as erect and free as they can. In the beginning wind instrument
class, where habits are established that will endure for years, special
attention to the posture of students is essential.

In their private practice, wind instrument players should stand whenever they can. Correct standing posture implies that the feet will be at a slight angle, that each foot will bear its half of the weight of the body, and that the weight will be equally distributed between the heels and the balls of the feet. The back will be straight, the head erect and facing forward. The arms will hang naturally from the shoulders without tension, except as required to hold the instrument in the proper playing position. If the performer must stand for some time, the weight of the body may be shifted slightly from foot to foot, or the position of the feet may be slightly altered. Slight body movements are appropriate to help reduce tensions.

The characteristics of good standing posture may be transferred to the seated position by sitting as far forward in the chair as possible. When seated, the weight of the body is carried by the chair but the carriage of the body is essentially the same. The feet will be flat on the floor, perhaps with one foot drawn slightly back of the other. The body will be carried erectly or inclined very slightly forward from the hips. The head will be straight, facing forward and held up proudly. The arms will retain their tension-free position.

Young students can be encouraged to adopt good posture habits by being provided with suitable equipment. Chairs for young players should be of a suitable size so that the children's feet will comfortably touch the floor. The seat of the chair should be flat rather than tilted and the back of the chair should be straight—although the back will not be used except during non-playing moments. In order to support the player properly and to enable him to learn good habits of posture, the chair should be constructed with legs at all four corners so that it cannot tip forward unexpectedly. Music stands should be adjustable so that music may be at or a bit below eye level for each student.

The teacher of a beginning class will find that he must constantly remind his students of good posture. He may do so most effectively by working with individuals. For most students, a brief comment or admonitory glance will suffice.

POSTURE:
HOLDING THE INSTRUMENT

The way in which an instrument is held and the manner in which it is brought to the lips are considerations of fundamental importance. Because instruments differ so widely, each has its own optimum position. These positions may be slightly modified to accommodate individual players or different models of instruments as long as the modifications do not increase the problems of performance.

Generally speaking, an instrument is held in the hands in such a way that the wrists and lower arms are free of strain. Any position that involves unnatural crooking of the wrists or elbows will set up tensions that affect finger dexterity and, perhaps, tone. Fingers are arched over keys and valve buttons so that the contact point is the ball of the finger in woodwind playing and the tip of the finger in the brasses. The movement of the fingers is always perfectly smooth if the arch of the fingers and the position of the wrist are maintained. Awkward positions of the elbows, either too close to the body or too extended, should be avoided.

When instruments are brought to the lips for the production of tone, the approach is straight-forward and natural. The head must never be taken to the instrument. Instead, the body and head are held erect, and the arms and hands bring the instrument up in the gentlest of lifting motions. The particular angle of the instrument to the floor or to the plane of the player's face will, of course, differ among the various instruments.

Particular pains must be taken with playing posture during the early stages of instruction so that inefficient and harmful attitudes will not become habitual. Posture is best taught by example and personal reminders.

BREATHING

The tone of a wind instrument depends upon adequate control and support of the breath, achieved most effectively through diaphragmatic breathing. Diaphragmatic breathing is perfectly natural for children. Their first breaths were diaphragmatic and they probably breathe properly most of the time without instruction; but when they have been made overly conscious of breathing, the natural up-and-down movement of the diaphragm is sometimes replaced by the more intricate movement of the shoulders and rib cage. Hence, correct breathing may perhaps be taught most effectively by indirection. In fact, it has been said that wind instrument teachers sometimes over-emphasize breathing to the detriment of their students and that all that is actually needed is a "thimbleful" of air!

The diaphragm is a large muscle running transversely across the body just below the lungs. As it is depressed, the lungs expand and take in large quantities of air, smoothly and easily. As the diaphragm is raised, air is forced out of the lungs, just as smoothly and easily. Evidence of diaphragmatic breathing will be noted by the slight expansion of the area just below the ribs and the absence of movement of the shoulders.

Beginning wind instrument students should be taught to inhale quickly, as if gasping in fright. The air should be taken in through the corners of the mouth—never through the instrument—and with the least possible disturbance of the embouchure. Exhalation must be done slowly so as to conserve the breath as long as possible. If it is necessary to practice breathing without using instruments, the exhalation should be between the teeth and tongue as in hissing so that some of the resistance of the instrument will be approximated. Many teachers also ask students to expel the air as if to bend a candle flame without extinguishing it.

Some teachers make routine the breathing process preparatory to making an attack with a five-step process done "by the counts." A four-beat silent measure is used to take these steps:

1. Inhale, using the diaphragm.
2. Hold the breath and set the embouchure.
3. Keep holding the breath and set the tongue.
4. Push the air from the diaphragm against the tongue.
5. (On beat 1 of the new measure) Release the tongue so that the air flows into the mouthpiece and the tone starts.

As skills develop, this five-step process is compressed into an instant just before the attack is made. This requires that the breath be taken very quickly.

All breathing should be done as inaudibly as possible, and all breathing should be done with a sense of proportion for the amount of time the breath must last. Usually children take in more breath than they need. They also tend to breathe at every rest, whether they need to or not.

Once students are able to play for more than a single measure in one breath they should be taught to maintain a steady flow of air regardless of the action of tongue or fingers. Melodic exercises, with definite phrase structure, are probably best for this work since the point of phrasal breathing may be better understood in the concrete than in the abstract.

Most notes in wind instrument music are stopped by halting the flow of air through the lips. Beginning students need practice in supporting the tone for its written duration and then, simply, ceasing to blow—without a slacking off of air pressure or a constriction of the throat or lips. The tone should not be stopped by placing the tongue against the back of the teeth or on the reed so that an unpleasant "tut" sound is heard. This faulty technique will always retard facility in articulation and will hinder development of tone quality. It might be said, in illustration, that to stop a tone one just begins to take a breath for the next one. The teacher may help his students by using a familiar conducting gesture—the cut-off with a lift.

In rapid passages, and in repeated staccato, the tone may sometimes be stopped with a rebounding stroke of the tongue. In such cases, the flow of air must remain constant as in playing sustained tones or legato passages. When extremely short notes, or notes surrounded by rests, are first introduced, it is important to review the use of the breath so that hard-won gains are not sacrificed.

10

Rhythm
and Reading

Students accepted into an instrumental music class are eager to begin playing their instruments. Their interest is extremely high. Therefore, it is a teacher's responsibility to maintain and increase their interest during the first year of study. Furthermore, children want to play something that they find musically satisfying—melodies they know and like and of which they may be proud. It is a teacher's responsibility to let them make music. If music-making can be accomplished only by rote procedures, no harm will be done, for *the prime motive for the study of music is to make music!*

As soon as students can play a few notes they should begin to play melodies. In the early development of instrumental music students, it is not at all important that they be able to read music. Even after the formal note-reading process has begun there will be many times when a wise teacher will permit students to play melodies with rhythmic content far beyond their "book-learning" level, if these melodies are within the limits of their fingering skill and embouchure development, and if they are songs the children know and love.

When music-reading procedures are initiated, the teacher will discover that rhythmic reading presents the greatest challenge. Note-reading—that is, the use of the correct fingering and embouchure setting in relation to staff notation—is much simpler. Consequently, the preparation for rhythmic reading must be started quite early in the series of lessons.

RHYTHM IS EVERYWHERE

Every normal human being has a natural sense of rhythm that may be developed by environment and training. The person trained in the music of Bach, Beethoven, and Brahms, upon hearing a *mariachi* band from Mexico for the first time, will probably become hopelessly lost and sit in amazed silence wondering how the musicians are able to feel such complicated rhythms. Yet to the Mexican the rhythms are perfectly simple because he *feels* them.

This feeling for rhythm, for regular pulsations and subdivision of pulses, is perfectly natural to the child. It is developed by unconscious observation of the world about him and becomes complicated and difficult only when it is isolated from normal human processes or represented by arbitrary symbols that do not look as rhythm sounds. Preparation for the reading of rhythmic notation, therefore, must proceed from natural impulses to move in rhythm and to respond to rhythmic stimuli by rote.

Teachers of general music in the elementary schools have long been aware of the value of rote approaches to learning rhythms, and the instrumental music teacher working in a school with a fine general music program is fortunate indeed, for his students will come to him with a background of meaningful experiences in singing and rhythmic activities. Before instituting any rhythmic work with his beginning classes the wise teacher will learn from the general music teacher in each of his schools the methods that have been employed in teaching rhythmic responses and rhythmic notation. He will then be able to use what his students have already learned and thereby avoid or minimize conflicts in terminology.

SOLVING THE PROBLEM
OF RHYTHMIC READING

Imagine a high school typing teacher saying to the thirty students in his class, "Turn to page 27 in your books. We are going to type this page. When I drop my arm, I want you all to start. You are to stay together in your typing and type each letter, make each space and shift, and type the last period at exactly the same time."

Would a typing teacher consider such a stunt impossible? Probably. But it is far less complicated than what is expected as a matter of course in a high school instrumental ensemble. A band or orchestra may have as many as 100 students using 15 to 17 different kinds of instruments. They stay together while reading, not from a single page, but from 26 to 32 completely different pages. This achievement is possible only when a thorough training in rhythmic response and rhythmic reading has been acquired.

In the early stages of the learning process children should learn their first melodies by rote, but there comes a time when the skills of rhythmic reading must be developed. To do it properly, the wise teacher will carefully integrate the reading process with the rote process. He will capitalize on the interest of the children in wanting to play new melodies that they have never had a chance to hear. And he will develop a system that will be as helpful and consistent as the system of phonetics is to the teacher of languages.

Some children will learn to read almost as though through a process of osmosis from their contact with rote songs and from playing melodies from notation. Others, however, will need to be shown the way through a carefully-developed plan by the teacher. The teacher must know how to approach every new rhythmic problem and have a proven, workable solution at his fingertips. These solutions can be very simple in the beginning stages and more complex as the student advances.

It is important that the new teacher develop and refine his system of teaching reading as soon as possible. If he fails to do so, he is likely to find himself continually teaching all music, even to his advanced students, by rote. The sooner a child can learn to read—after he has learned to produce a sound and hear what he is doing—the sooner he will more fully enjoy making music and become independent of his teacher. The problems and frustrations of the teacher will be reduced. No longer will it be necessary to stop every few measures to find out "how the music goes." Instead, children and teacher will experience the thrill of performing music in an acceptable manner at the first reading.

A SYSTEM OF TEACHING
RHYTHMIC READING

Many systems have been devised to teach the reading of rhythms. Any of these methods may be considered satisfactory if it works and if it does not violate the basic principles of teaching. The material that follows here outlines the most important elements of a system that has been found successful in the teaching of hundreds of elementary school children.

Inexperienced children find it difficult to keep in mind the particular

counts of a measure, 1–2–3–4. It is far simpler to have them count only
the value of the note or the rest.

This may be done in such a way that the student develops a feeling
for the pulsation of beats. It is related to what the children have learned
in general music—that one can walk to the pulsation of quarter notes.
The instrumental music teacher might even have his students march
around the room reciting the proper counts.

As the students advance the teacher may wish to have them tap the
toes of one foot as they play to indicate the pulse. Foot-tapping is recommended for wind instrument players but not necessarily for players of
piano or the stringed or percussion instruments, who should count aloud
as they play. Foot-tapping is a great aid to the student, but it is of even
more help to the teacher, who is thus able to observe from the movement of the feet whether the child is thinking properly.

Foot-tapping should be carefully taught. Each pulsation must start
when the foot touches the floor and continue until the foot has been
raised and returned to the floor. The lifting motion should be so exact
that the mid-point of the pulse is precisely marked by the top of the foot
movement. The foot directions may be indicated by arrows pointing
down and up.

By stressing evenness of foot-tapping, the teacher lays down the
foundation for playing eighth notes. When paired eighth notes first
occur, the teacher merely tells the students to play the first one when the
foot touches the floor and the second one when the foot reaches the
top of its beat. Sometimes it is easier for young students to understand
paired eighth notes if they say "part-ner, part-ner." Once the process
has become fairly secure they should be taught to say "1-&-2-&."

In the above example eighth notes have been written in two ways. The students should be shown the difference as they will find instrumental music printed one way and music in many song books printed the other way. It should be explained that in instrumental music the notes are generally grouped by counts because it is easier for the performer to find the beats within each measure. To demonstrate, the teacher may write the following on the chalkboard without letting the children see what is being written.

The example should be covered with the teacher's arm or a large piece of paper. The notation is revealed for an instant and the children are asked to identify the number of notes on the board. Only by chance will someone give the correct answer. Then the teacher places another example on the board.

Again, the example should be shown only for an instant. Immediately, most of the class will respond with the word, "Seven!"

The dotted quarter note appears to be the biggest stumbling block for young classes. While it may be played correctly by rote, as in "America," it will be incorrectly interpreted in an unfamiliar piece. This is because the thought process and the feeling is different for a dotted quarter note. When properly taught and thoroughly understood by the students, the remaining rhythmic figures are fairly easy to teach. Students who do not understand the dotted quarter note are almost on a learning plateau.

The figure may be taught in steps. To start, a complete musical phrase is placed on the chalkboard, since a complete phrase will provide a feeling for the whole.

The teacher then calls different students to the board to write the necessary items in these steps:

1. Write the count under the notes.
2. Draw the proper down and up arrows under the notes.
3. Draw a circle around the complete second count, including the counting symbols and the arrows.

4. Draw a dotted line, from top to bottom, to separate the first half of the second count from the last half of the second count.

5. Ask how many counts each note receives (1, ½, ½, 2).

6. Tie the first note to the second note.

7. Ask how many counts the first and second notes, tied together, receive (1½).

8. Ask how many down taps of the foot the quarter note tied to the eighth note receives (2).

9. Develop the concept that a quarter note tied to an eighth note receives *2 down taps, but only 1½ counts!*

10. Show how a dotted quarter is an abbreviation for a quarter and eighth note tied together, just as a dotted half note (previously learned) is an abbreviation for a half and a quarter tied together and just as "Ill." is an abbreviation for "Illinois."

When the chalkboard work has been completed it should look like this:

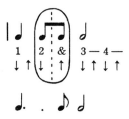

This explanation, like all other explanations, will not be understood by all students the first time it is presented, nor will all who seem to have grasped it remember until the next lesson. The teacher will need to be patient and to take time to review again and again. One of the greatest joys a teacher can experience comes when a student looks up, his face alight, and says, "I've got it!"

Sixteenth notes are fairly easy to teach. Using the foot-tap as the basis, and starting with eighth notes in a complete phrase, grouped sixteenths are developed in this way:

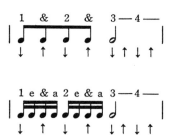

Other common figures may be introduced in a similar manner:

In all presentations involving sixteenth notes, the expression "1-e-&-a" (pronounced "One-ee-and-uh") is preferred because it is directly related to the counting of eighth notes and can be used in many patterns without confusion. The numbers always refer to the beginning of the count and the "and" to the last half of the count. Systems using the syllable "tu" (as in "1-ta-tu-ta") tend to be confusing since some students hear "tu" as "two."

In teaching triplets, the downward movement of the foot is more important than the upward movement, and, upon a single stress, the feeling for three subdivisions is developed. This is usually quite easy for children since many of their most popular fun songs have a triplet feeling. In developing counting procedures, the syllable "and" must not be used because it is reserved for defining the half-way point. Rather, triplets should be counted as "1-la-le, 2-la-le" (pronounced "lah-lee").

"Cut-time" and 6/8 time (when the eighth note receives one count) present no real problems as long as one important concept is established —that any kind of note may be given one count. The tendency of children to fix on the concept of the quarter note as the only possible count-note can be avoided by reviewing earlier pieces, playing them twice as fast as before so that, for example, 4/4 becomes 2/2. The children will enjoy the review and will be amazed at the ease with which they can play lessons that were once quite difficult.

Six-eight time with two counts to a measure often causes difficulty. The problem may be attacked two ways. One is to have the students play the music with six counts to a measure and gradually increase the speed until they are playing in two counts to a measure. The other, and probably the better, method is to teach students to read 6/8 time "in two," by relating the unknown to the known.

The teacher should first explain that 6/8 time may be played slowly or fast. If the children have had experience in the slow method, the teacher may have them count "1-2-3-4-5-6" as he conducts. As the beat becomes faster, the students find they cannot distinguish the separate points of the beats and end in wild confusion. The teacher then repeats the exercise. But this time, when the tempo begins to become difficult, he changes his beat into a pattern of two while the class continues to count in six. The students will be quick to respond to questions and disclose that they observed the change from six to two, that they found it quite easy to stay together in counting, that they were counting three numbers to a beat, and that this was like the counting of triplets.

Students should be made aware of the fact that the signature of ⁶⁄₈ time at a fast tempo is really 2/ ♩ , and that at slow tempos it is 6/ ♪ . Young students can usually remember that the upper numeral in a signature indicates "counts-per-measure," but they often forget that the bottom numeral indicates the kind of note that receives a count. Many teachers help students understand this by substituting a note for the lower numeral of the time signature.

The final step in teaching ⁶⁄₈ in two is to relate the unknown to the known, using the counting syllables the children learned for triplets.

MNEMONIC AIDS

Sometimes effective short-cuts may be taken by the use of such expressions as "part-ners" for paired eighths, "Mis-sis-sip-pi" for grouped sixteenths, or "hap-pi-ly, hap-pi-ly" for sixteenth note triplets.

These devices are often very helpful in teaching rhythmic patterns because the act of saying the syllables is closely related to the actual playing of the notes when superimposed on a good awareness of the counts in each measure as well as basic rhythmic patterns. They must all be as familiar as common words in the child's vocabulary. The teacher must see that they are learned in meaningful ways and without the use of any aids that need to be "unlearned."

Mnemonic aids, helpful in teaching rhythms, are deleterious when used with the degrees of the staff or the order of sharps and flats in key signatures. They are easily confused and applied to the wrong problems. "All cows eat grass," "Go down and eat breakfast," and "Every good boy does fine" trip equally smoothly off the tongue—no one is preferable to the others. In the time it takes a child to recite one of these phrases and to decide which word applies to the note or key he wants to identify, he could call off half a dozen notes or keys learned by direct methods and avoid the possible choice of the wrong phrase.

NOTE-READING PROBLEMS

The young teacher is often surprised to find that after much hard work his students do not know the names of the notes when they appear on the staff. His first reaction may be to blame the students for their lack of memory. After all, he thinks, he had taught them carefully when notation was introduced and the students seemed to understand. With a little more experience, the teacher will learn that the lapse was his fault. Perhaps he had merely introduced the note names without making the experience meaningful. Perhaps he had drilled on the names for a short time and assumed that they would be remembered. The experienced teacher knows that learning does not happen this way.

When the time comes for the teaching of note names—after the children have been playing by rote for some time—the teacher might make this kind of introduction:

"Boys and girls, even though I know all of your names very well, I want you to tell me your names again to help us learn something new about music." When the students have recited their names, he continues, "Now, why do you suppose you all have different names? Why aren't all the boys called Ricky and all the girls called Martha?" Invariably, a student will reply, "So we can be told apart."

"Very good," the teacher responds. "You already know a little about notes because we have talked about them and you have used them with your singing teacher, Miss Jones. Now I am going to tell you something important about notes. They have names, just like people. And that is so that we can tell them apart when we talk about them. After all, they look and sound different, so why shouldn't they be called differently?"

The teacher can then introduce a few notes, using the chalkboard. He must be very careful to introduce only a few at a time. It is important that they be written with great care. Notes in spaces should touch the lines above and below exactly; notes on lines should be of the same size and bisected exactly by the line. Otherwise students become confused. The concept of "on the line" can lead a child to see a note only partially filling a space as "sitting on the line." The difference between notes *in* spaces and *on* lines must be explained carefully. This is particularly true because it may be the first time in the children's lives that the word *on* means "bisected by." In their writing classes, they have learned to put all letters "on the lines," meaning "in the space but touching the line and not going beyond the line except for letters with tails."

Young teachers frequently neglect to review note names and to provide adequate drill on them. Recitation on note names during rest periods should be augmented by concentrated drill by the whole class. A "Name-that-note Contest" will be profitable and pleasant; it may be conducted by asking students to identify notes at random as they are pointed out on the chalkboard.

Children need to be able to identify notes and to associate staff notation with fingerings. These are not the same processes and are not necessarily learned together. Many students can do one and not the other; frequent drill in both kinds of response is essential.

Drill in note naming is but a means to an end. It must never become a complete lesson in itself but must be integrated with all instruction. Short, intensive drills in every class session, done pleasantly and with a variety of approaches, will produce excellent results.

11

Evaluation
and
Communication

Evaluation is a continuing process in human life. In the world of education, the teacher's evaluation of student progress becomes the guide for
decisions by students, parents, and other teachers. It is a responsibility
that cannot be brushed off lightly. Even more difficult is the evaluation
to which a conscientious teacher continually subjects *himself*.

THE ASSIGNMENT OF GRADES

In most school systems the in-
structor's assessment of student progress is reported by some kind of
grade. Some schools express the evaluation in terms of letter grades—
"A" for work of highest quality, "C" for supposedly average work, "E"
or "F" for failing work. Some schools use the initial letters of descriptive
words—"E" for excellent, "G" for good, "F" for failure. Still other schools
insist that all students be graded according to a numerical scale running
from 0 to 100, 100 being the grade given for the very best work and,
perhaps, 70 being given as the lowest passing grade.

All these devices have the advantage of being easy to record and compare. They have the great *dis*advantage of being taken to represent too much, allowing too little room for the reporting of fine judgments. One of the disadvantages of single-character grades can be diminished by the use of one or more subsidiary letters or numerals. This type of reporting acknowledges the quality of work with a letter and the quality of citizenship with a numeral. A student receiving a grade of "C-3" would be understood to have done only average work ("C") and to have been deficient in paying attention or some other phase of classroom discipline ("3"). When accompanied by additional comments from the teacher, such grades are often more meaningful to parents. Some schools use combination grades with a restricted vocabulary of descriptive words so that "A-Medium" would represent the work of a student who is superior but still not, in the teacher's opinion, working up to his capacity or exhibiting good citizenship traits in the classroom.

Perhaps the best way to report student progress in such a complex subject as instrumental music is to employ a report form similar to the one reproduced on page 79. Even though the data on the report might need to be reduced to a single letter grade, the instructor will be much more accurate if he can have a set of standards and evaluative categories before him.

This evaluation form was developed by the instrumental music teachers in the elementary schools of Ann Arbor, Michigan, and has been revised from time to time. It is used twice a year—at the end of each semester. The report is prepared in triplicate. The first copy is sent to the parents, the second retained in the student's permanent folder. The third copy of the first semester report is kept by the teacher to aid him in preparing the next evaluation. At the end of the second semester the third copy is sent to the office of the music coordinator to be forwarded the next fall to the student's new instrumental music teacher in the sixth or seventh grade. All reports are checked by the building principals, whose evaluation of the evaluation is often of great help to the teacher.

If it is not feasible to report to parents in the detailed manner of the Ann Arbor reporting system, a file of similar reports for the benefit of the instrumental music teacher is still recommended. Instrumental music teachers normally meet far more children each week than do most elementary school teachers and meet them for only short periods of time. The creation of a developmental record for each student will be invaluable in responding to parents' questions, in forecasting enrollments for advanced organizations, and in evaluating the teacher's own work.

ANN ARBOR PUBLIC SCHOOLS

Elementary Instrumental Music Report

NAME_____   _____SEMESTER, 19___

SCHOOL_____   CLASSROOM TEACHER_____

GRADE_____   CLASS: Beginning_____, Advanced _____

MUSICIANSHIP

The check in the first line of squares indicates the student's performance in relation to the entire class. The check in the second line shows the teacher's estimate of the student's ability in music. The check in the third line shows the student's progress in relation to this estimate of his musical ability.

Comparative Performance	Poor	Fair	Average	Good	Superior
Estimate of Ability	Poor	Fair	Average	Good	Superior
Performance vs. Ability	Poor	Fair	Average	Good	Superior

For each ability used in playing an instrument a letter shows the student's achievement in relation to his own musical capacity: G (good) for achievement at the level of his capacity, F (fair) for achievement somewhat below his capacity, P (poor) for achievement seriously below his capacity.

_____ Tone quality

_____ Knowledge of fingerings

_____ Reading of note names

_____ Sense of rhythm

_____ Sense of pitch

_____ Breath control

_____ Playing position (position of hands, instrument, embouchure, posture)

CITIZENSHIP

The comments below indicate the student's attitudes and cooperation in instrumental music.

_____ Preparation of lessons

_____ Attention in class

_____ Response to instruction

_____ Care of equipment

_____ Courtesy

_____ Cooperation

_____ Promptness

_____ Attendance with instrument, music

A conference with the parent
is always welcomed.

_____
Instrumental Music Teacher

Phone:_____

Additional comments, if any, on reverse side

GATHERING DATA
FOR REPORTS

No report is better than the data used in preparing it, and the instrumental music teacher must be particularly careful in the assembly of his data since his subject does not lend itself to daily or weekly written examinations or to the establishment of fixed proficiency levels. Therefore, he must assemble data over a reasonably long period of time and in a variety of situations. He must also avoid being influenced by factors not truly part of the learning process in instrumental music. Personality factors should never intrude.

Honesty in grading is essential. Far too often, high school students choose careers in music only to discover that they have no real talent. If their grades in music have been kept at an artificially high level by being based on regularity of attendance or willingness to do non-musical tasks, the students have been misled by their teachers. Or if a talented child has been discouraged because the grading standard is overly rigid or too heavily weighted for appearance, attendance, and other extraneous factors, his life has been made poorer because of the inaccuracy of a teacher's evaluative procedures.

The report of student progress should reflect information gleaned in the normal order of class meetings and in periodic special and more formal examinations. Using some of the devices discussed in Chapter 8 (under "Rest Periods that Work"), the teacher can hear every child every time the class meets. He should not make an obvious effort to record grades on these occasions, however, but remember (and write down after class) exactly what each student did and how each effort was related to earlier efforts. The reason that this part of the lesson should not be formalized by the display of a grade-book is that the final grade should express evaluations of the student's ability to do work in normal as well as special situations, and the presence of a grade-book always makes a situation "special" in the eyes of a student. Then, too, the "rest periods that work" are most effective as learning situations when they grow naturally out of the needs of the lesson and are conducted in a reasonably relaxed manner.

The teacher can also gain much information about his students if he will walk among them during the class. Many attributes of performance and behavior will be more apparent when the class is working as a unit.

From time to time, the instrumental music teacher may wish to set up a rather formal testing procedure that will present a challenge to his students. This might well be done after a significant series of learnings has taken place and should always be preceded by adequate notification and ample opportunity for review—this because the teacher's primary job is to teach, not to test. Such a test, in a clarinet class, might cover all fingerings in the chalumeau register before the "break" is introduced. Students would be expected to know all fingerings (notation-to-fingering, fingering-to-notation, note names, and staff degrees), be able to play all these notes with satisfactory tone quality, and have complete command of all rhythmic notation introduced to that point. The instructor might wish to establish definite standards and to inform the students of those standards so that they will know exactly what is expected of them.

STUDENT SELF-EVALUATION

One of the constant dangers in teaching instrumental music is the tendency to be inaccurate in the estimation of student achievement. Another danger is to assume that only the instructor is capable of making judgments. Actually, students are often more alert and discerning than teachers think they are. Their alertness and discernment may be encouraged by the institution of a system of challenges in which they make the decisions. The challenge system is similar to the try-out system (in which the teacher makes the decision) but is conducted in such a way that the students accept the responsibility. Many such systems have been devised, but the most successful, considering all the goals of the instrumental music class, are those that permit the students to vote. Challenges work most smoothly if done from the "top of the class"; that is, when the second in line is given the first opportunity to better his position. If he fails, he is then subject to the challenge of the third, and possibly the fourth, student, so that all may have an opportunity to progress upward.

Even though a system of challenges might be unfeasible, students should learn to evaluate their own work and the work of their classmates. They will enjoy seeing the progress made by their fellows and will learn a great deal that will help their own performance by noting the strong and weak points demonstrated by others in the class.

A record of student progress may be kept on a wall chart with check marks or stars indicating successive levels of mastery. The teacher and his students will enjoy watching the chart fill up as the members of the class conquer the problems of learning to play well, and each child will be able to evaluate his rate of progress against that of his classmates.

TEACHER SELF-EVALUATION

Every teacher must evaluate his work, as it is being done and later when he can review the entire lesson period. He must do so because the success of the instrumental music program in his school depends more upon his skill as a teacher than it does upon the native talent of the students in his class. Only by constant re-evaluation of all his methods can he improve and thereby improve his program.

During the course of a lesson, the teacher must be attentive to signs of restlessness, inattention, boredom, and confusion. The fine teacher learns to read the eyes and hands of his students. If eyes are focused on the teacher or on the music, all is well; if they are wandering, he had better find an activity that will restore the attention of the class. If hands are moving aimlessly about the instruments, the teacher knows that the minds controlling the hands are also wandering, and he will quickly introduce an activity that will stimulate renewed interest. The fine teacher remembers that students can look without seeing, listen without hearing, and play without thinking. He will constantly be alert to the incursions of boredom and be quick to depart from his lesson plan if he sees that he has not taken the children with him.

After every class, the fine teacher re-examines himself. He asks which parts of the lesson were most successful and why; which parts were least successful and why: "Was this a good class? Did the children enjoy themselves? Was the experience meaningful? Did I choose my words properly? Could I have been more stimulating? Or was I so over-stimulating that the children became nervous?"

When lessons go badly, as they sometimes do for every teacher, he will ask whether it was his fault or the atmospheric conditions or the interruption of a fire drill or the lassitude that comes from too little sleep. The hardest part of self-evaluation is being honest with oneself. The successful teacher admits his faults and undertakes their correction and elimination. The healthy teacher does not brood about his failures but takes steps to see that they never occur again.

COMMUNICATION PROBLEMS

Instrumental music, perhaps more than many other subjects, requires a three-way attack: Child, teacher, and parent must all understand what is going on and why. Many of the failures of children in instrumental music classes are due to the lack of communication between teacher and parent. When parents do not understand that home practice is needed, that regularity of attendance with the instrument is essential, that instruments requires a special kind of care, the child suffers.

Many of these problems can be avoided by the establishment of firm policies reported to parents in the letter announcing that the beginning class has been selected. Later reminders by briefly written notes are often helpful, as are telephone calls. If a boy habitually forgets his instrument and the teacher can satisfy himself that the teaching is not at fault, a telephone call to the parents will often suffice. The call should be tactful even though the parent (who often is misinformed or has not understood the problem) forgets to be tactful. If the telephone call fails to produce satisfactory results, and if it appears that the boy is in danger of being dropped from the class, it is often wise to ask the boy to write a note to his parents:

Dear Mother and Dad,

I have forgotten my instrument three times. If I forget it one more time I will be dropped from the instrumental music class at school.

Harry

The letter is then signed by the instrumental music teacher, the classroom teacher, and the principal. It is taken home, signed by the parents, and returned to the instrumental music teacher.

This procedure may sound severe. But in the light of all that the public schools and the instrumental music class are expected to do, it is perfectly appropriate. Harry has a problem—the failure to accept responsibility. Everyone who works with Harry now knows about it and can help him get to class with his instrument, even if it means sending it to him in a taxi! The lesson Harry learns in this way may make a great deal of difference to him as he continues through school and into the world of adulthood. To have dropped him summarily from the instrumental music class would have deprived him of one more opportunity to learn about music and about the responsibilities all human beings must shoulder.

12

The
Woodwind
Instruments

The woodwind instruments are, in simplest terms, cylindrical or conical tubes, perforated at intervals so that scales may be played, provided with keywork to open and close the perforations, and furnished at one end with a tone-generating mechanism. The tone generator permits a stream of air to strike against a surface or an edge so that the column of air inside the instrument is made to vibrate. The length of the vibrating column of air determines the pitch of the tone.

The keywork is so arranged that the principal diatonic notes are fingered with the first three fingers and the thumb of the left hand and the first three fingers of the right hand. The two little fingers control keys that extend the range or produce chromatics. The left hand is held nearer the tone generator. Because all woodwind instruments follow this principle it is possible to derive a chart of diatonic fingerings more or less common to the group. The chart on page 86 must *not* be considered a universal fingering chart since it does not indicate the changes of fingerings required to move into the various registers or the alternate chromatic and diatonic fingerings and resonance fingerings.

Since the pitch of a tone is determined by the distance from the tone generator to the first open tone-hole, the effect of closing three tone-holes is to make the fourth hole in the series establish the pitch. Because of this, chromatic fingerings usually require sharping a diatonic fingering by opening a tone-hole midway between two diatonic tone-holes with a key or lever. This principle can best be observed by a study of the clarinet.

The prototypes of the woodwinds produced only the tones of a single octave. As the instruments developed, provisions were made to extend the range by forcing the air column inside the instrument to vibrate at higher frequencies and in parts rather than in wholes. The achievement of range extension gave each of the instruments several registers using the basic fingerings. In the flute, the lowest octave provides the basic fingerings; the second octave, with essentially the same fingerings, is "overblown"—the air stream from the lips is increased in speed and intensity, and its angle is changed. In the oboe and saxophone, the first and second octaves differ only in the opening of a speaker or octave key. The bassoon uses many of the lowest tones in its second octave by opening a whisper key. The clarinet functions differently; it "overblows" a twelfth and then a sixth for its two upper registers and has an intermediate register of four notes known as the "throat register."

Because speaker openings are fixed and cannot always be at the proper dividing point of the air column, most woodwinds have been provided with auxiliary speaker keys. Some tones are improved in quality and intonation by "half-holing" with the first finger. In the extreme upper octave of the flute, the "speaker" moves along the length of the flute as "cross-fingerings" are used. Many of the problems encountered by inexperienced players result from incorrect fingerings that fail to employ the right speaker mechanism for the upper registers.

WOODWIND
FINGERING SYSTEMS

The modern flute, clarinet, and saxophone all employ various forms of the Boehm key system. The differences among them are not great. Only the flute and the clarinet are commonly referred to as being Boehm system instruments in fingering charts and other data.

Each of the double-reed instruments exists in Europe in two fingering systems. Since the differences in fingering systems are accompanied by differences in acoustical design, the reeds also differ and cannot be interchanged. The oboe systems are called "military" and "conservatory," the latter being preferred in the United States. The bassoon systems are called French or German (or Heckel), the latter again preferred here.

BASIC WOODWIND FINGERINGS

		Left Hand					Right Hand			
	0	Thumb	1	2	3	Little	4	5	6	Little
1. Pre-band Instruments	D	C	B	A	G	—	F	E	D	C
2. Oboe (Lowest octave, 2nd octave with speaker)	—	(Speaker key)	B	A	G	G# B♮ / E♭ B♭	F#	E	D	C# E♭ / C
3. Flute (First two octaves)	C#	(B♮, B♭)	C* / B	A	G	G#	F	E	D	C / C#
4. Saxophone (First two octaves)	C#	(Speaker key)	B	A	G	G# / B♭ B♮ C#	F	E	D	D# / -C
5. Clarinet (Clarion register)	—	C	B	A	G	G# C / B♮ C#	F	E	D	D# C / C# B♭
6. Clarinet (Altissimo register)	—	(Register key)	(Open or half-hole as speaker)	F#	E	F / —	D	C#	—	(X) / —
7. Clarinet (Chalumeau register)	G	F	F#* / E	D	C	C# F / E F#	B♭	A	G	G# / F# , G♭
8. Bassoon (Notes on bass staff)	F	—	E	D	C	(C#)	B♮	A	G♭ / G	F / A♭

1. Chromatics are possible on pre-band instruments. For example, F-sharp is fingered 123050 or 123006.
2. Oboe C, add 4 to B; B-flat, add 4 to A; F, raise E with 5½ or lower F-sharp with 6. C-sharp, D, D-sharp in second octave require half-holing of 1. C-sharp to G, use thumb octave key; above G-sharp use side octave key.
3. Flute F-sharp, T123006; B-flat, T100400. In second octave, raise 1 for D and D-sharp. ALWAYS HOLD D-SHARP KEY OPEN except for the D's and for low C, C-sharp, and some tones in third octave.
4. Saxophone: F-sharp, 123050; B-flat, 100400 or sharp A with side key. C, 020000, or sharp B with side key.
5. Clarinet, middle: F-sharp, TR123050; B-flat, TR100400 or sharp A.
6. Clarinet, altissimo: Use open 1 for register key. Add D-sharp key for resonance above D-sharp. High E-flat similar to low B and middle F-sharp; high F-sharp similar to low D and middle A; high G, TR020450x.
7. Clarinet, low: Like middle clarinet register but without register key--transpose down a twelfth. Throat tones: G-sharp, an L-shaped key; A, a small key just above 1; B-flat, A plus the register key.
8. Bassoon; B-flat, sharp A with LH 3; C-sharp, sharp C with left thumb; E-flat, sharp D with left thumb; Half-hole F-sharp and G at top of staff.
* Flute and clarinet in chalumeau register: C or F-sharp without the thumb; B or E with the thumb.

CARE OF
THE WOODWINDS

The keywork of a woodwind instrument provides for the covering of tone-holes that cannot be reached or sealed by the fingers in normal playing position—that is, the chromatic tones, the lower and upper extensions of the fundamental diatonic scale of the instrument, and tone-holes that are larger than the tips of the fingers. The keywork is mounted on a series of hinges and pivot screws on which the keys turn. Each key has a cup into which a pad is inserted to make an air-tight seal against the edges of the tone-hole. On the other side of the hinge from the cup is a foot that regulates the height of the key in its open position. Keys are held open or closed by needle springs or flat springs. Tone-holes may be opened or closed at considerable distances from the operating fingers by means of linkages among sets of keys, by levers, or, in the case of the bassoon, by rods running through the instrument.

The keywork is extremely delicate and should be treated with great care. An almost unnoticeable bend in a hinge may cause binding or a leak at a tone-hole. Some of the hinges are double—one running inside another—so that even a slight dent from contact with the sharp edge of a music stand can impair the action. The pads are made of plastic or of felt covered with fine skin; they can be easily torn and are particularly vulnerable to moisture from saliva in the instrument and to excessive key oil. When pads no longer furnish air-tight closures, instruments do not respond on tones below the damaged pad.

Most repair work on the keys of woodwind instruments should be done by a competent repairman although the installation of clarinet pads is not particularly difficult. When young students have trouble that seems to indicate some malfunction of the keywork, the instructor should ask them to play a descending scale in long tones. This will often locate the defective key. Sometimes problems of embouchure, reed, or mouthpiece cause symptoms similar to those of faulty keywork. The instructor should then finger the instrument as the student plays. This is quite easily done on the flute, saxophone, or bassoon. To test a clarinet or oboe in this way, the body of the instrument should be rotated 90 degrees so that the teacher can manipulate the keys as the student plays.

The keywork of woodwind instruments used by beginning students normally requires no oiling. When oil must be applied, single drops of high-grade key oil should be placed (by the teacher) at friction points with the tip of a toothpick. Over-oiling can lead to damaged pads.

All woodwinds must be protected from sudden or great changes of temperature. Many beginners' instruments, although "woodwinds," are made of plastics or of hard rubber. These should be protected from high temperatures. They are sometimes also vulnerable to chipping. The manufacturer's suggestions for the care of instruments should be observed.

The inner surfaces of woodwinds must be perfectly smooth and clean. After every usage, the bore should be thoroughly dried with an appropriate cleaning tool—a cloth on a rod for the flute, a chamois swab for the clarinet, saxophone, and bassoon, a pheasant feather for the oboe. Dirt may also collect on the tone-holes and pad seats. It may be removed by wiping with a feather or lintless cloth—but very, very gently.

Much of the damage to woodwind instruments occurs while they are in their cases. Music books, music stands, and other items should never be carried in cases, nor should cases be subjected to pressure that can be transmitted to the instrument. Cases should be securely locked to prevent accidental opening that would permit the instrument to fall to the ground.

ASSEMBLING
WOODWIND INSTRUMENTS

The joints of woodwind instruments are not difficult to put together except that care must be taken not to damage keywork in the process. Generally speaking, it is best to hold a joint where there are no keys. When this cannot be done, the joint should be held in the palm of the hand, the thumb and the lowest joint of the first finger being held nearly parallel to the body of the instrument. Pressure against keys and posts must be avoided.

The clarinet, oboe, saxophone, and bassoon have bridge keys connecting the keywork of one joint with the keywork of another. In assembling these instruments, the upper portion of the bridge key must be raised so that it cannot collide with the lower portion. The two halves of a bridge key then slide together readily. When the joints are assembled properly, bridge keys will be exactly in line. If they are not, tone-holes will not close properly.

Except for the flute, the tenons of woodwind instruments are fitted with corks to provide a tight seal. The corks should be greased occasionally with cork grease or petroleum jelly since a dry cork has a tendency to shrink and to be torn. When inserting a tenon into its receiver, a gentle twisting motion and an easy downward push will do the least damage. Care must be taken that the two joints are perfectly in line.

The following list of the names of woodwind instrument joints is arranged in the order in which they should be taken from the case and added one to another. When taking the instrument apart, the order is reversed:

Flute: Body, head joint, foot joint

Clarinet: Left-hand (upper) joint, right-hand (lower) joint, barrel joint, bell joint, mouthpiece, ligature, reed

Oboe: Left-hand (upper) joint, right-hand (lower) joint, bell, reed

Saxophone: Body, gooseneck, mouthpiece, ligature, reed

Bassoon: Butt (or boot), wing (tenor or short or right-hand) joint, bass (long) joint, bell (to the butt joint), bocal (or gooseneck—to the top of the wing joint), reed

Players of reed instruments should soak their reeds while putting their instruments together. If they soak the reeds in their mouths there is little chance of damaging the reeds (and less chance of desultory conversation).

WOODWIND
TONE PRODUCTION

Beginning flutists should be introduced to tone production by use of the head joint alone with the following instructions (to be amplified by demonstration):

Place the embouchure plate in the hollow of the chin just below the red part of the lower lip, holding the head joint in the left hand with the open end of the joint to the right. Permit the fleshy part of the lower lip to overhang the embouchure hole for about a fourth of the hole's diameter. Form the lips as if to say "pooh." Now begin to expel the breath very easily, pulling the corners of the mouth back and down until the opening between the lips is small enough to enable a tone to speak. The size of the aperture between the lips should be no larger than will allow a pencil point to be inserted.

The young flutist must learn to conserve breath by making the air stream as narrow as possible, directing the center of the stream against the outer edge of the embouchure hole so that the stream will be split in two almost-equal parts. This angle will be altered to enable movement into other registers—lower and into the head joint for the lowest octave, higher and over the edge of the embouchure plate for the highest octave. These movements are accompanied by upward or downward movements of the upper lips, slight changes in the position of the lower jaw, and changes in tension at the corners of the mouth. The correct combination of aperture size, air stream intensity and angle, and lip tension will produce the distinctive flute tone—centered, free of breathiness, and capable of projection.

By closing the open end of the head joint with the palm of the right hand, the beginner will be able to produce a fundamental and its twelfth to learn the differences of embouchure setting and air stream intensity.

The clarinet embouchure should be introduced with the mouthpiece alone with these directions (and demonstrations):

Roll the red portion of the lower lip slightly over the lower teeth. Place the reed on this cushion so that approximately half an inch of reed is inside the mouth. Drop the upper teeth onto the top of the mouthpiece firmly. Close the lips around the mouthpiece as if closing a purse with a drawstring. Pull the chin down and point it. Press up against the upper teeth with the mouthpiece. In this position, start a stream of air through the mouthpiece with the syllable "too."

As soon as the basic embouchure has been established, the instrument should be assembled and the G or F above middle C introduced. The right thumb must be in position under the thumb rest so that the clarinet is pushed up against the upper teeth. This upward pressure is essential for a good tone and cannot be easily developed with the mouthpiece alone.

The saxophone embouchure differs from the clarinet embouchure only in that the mouthpiece enters the mouth more horizontally and the pressure of the lower jaw is reduced. Too much pressure will destroy the distinctive saxophone tone, but too little yields a raucous sound. The throat should be kept open and the shape of the lips round.

The position of the reed is determined by responsiveness, but a general rule is to place reed and mouthpiece in the lips so that the point where reed and mouthpiece meet is just outside the fleshy, red portion of the lower lip. Quite a bit more mouthpiece must be taken in the mouth than in clarinet playing; this amount increases as reeds and mouthpieces become larger in the lower reeds.

The oboe embouchure is formed by placing the reed on the center of the lower lip without rolling the lip over the teeth. The reed should extend about three eighths of an inch into the mouth beyond the inner edge of the lip. The upper lip is brought down on the reed. Both lips are then pulled slightly into the mouth, taking the reed with them. All pressure on the reed comes from the lips alone, which are slightly pursed so that the air stream is directed into the slit between the blades of the reed with no bunching of chin muscles or distention of the cheeks. Since both blades of the reed must be free to vibrate, the reed must lie well within the mouth and the lips must be perfectly even. The chin is pulled down and pointed.

The oboe embouchure is perhaps the most tiring for beginners, at least among the woodwind instruments. Frequent rest periods are as necessary for young oboists as for young cornetists.

In forming the bassoon embouchure, the upper and lower lips are drawn slightly over the teeth and the reed is then inserted between the lips so that approximately a quarter of an inch of reed is free inside the mouth. The lips are then pursed around the reed, and the chin is pointed. The lower jaw should be drawn back and down so that an overbite of about a quarter of an inch is formed and the upper lip comes closer to the first wire than does the lower lip. The teeth are kept widely apart.

Using the reed alone, the beginner should experiment with the position until, by moving the reed back into the mouth and blowing against it, he can produce the distinctive "double crow" with its high and low overtones. When this position is found, it must be used when the reed is placed on the bocal and the beginner tries to make his first bassoon tone. Oboe reeds also may be made to "crow" and the point at which the crow occurs should be taken as the starting point for the first oboe tone.

WOODWIND TONGUING

Tonguing on the flute is quite like tonguing on a brass instrument. The tongue is directed at a spot just above the upper edge of the upper teeth so that it strikes against the gum. The movement of the tongue is a withdrawal from this position to permit the flow of air through the lips. Movement of the tongue in all woodwind playing should be done without altering the embouchure or the position of the instrument on or in the lips. Tongue strokes should be as short and precise as possible and should not entail movement of the base of the tongue or in the muscles below the chin.

The reed instruments are tongued by withdrawing the tongue from a point on the reed. Only a small bit of the tip of the tongue should engage a small bit of the surface of the tip of the reed. The tongue should not strike into the tip of the reed. The double reeds usually respond best when the tongue touches one of the corners of the reed rather than the entire width of the blade.

SELECTING REEDS
FOR BEGINNERS

Reeds for beginning clarinetists and saxophonists should be of medium strength or the next lower strength. Young players who have used extremely soft reeds have enjoyed success *as beginners* but at a sacrifice of later proficiency. A soft reed will respond to almost any kind of embouchure and encourage the development of poor embouchure habits.

Double reeds should also be of medium strength. They must be soaked in water, to the depth of the vibrating surfaces, for five to ten minutes before being played.

Young students will need to be cautioned about caring for their reeds. Reeds should be soaked in the mouth for about five minutes before being played and should be dried after use. Reeds that are cracked, chipped, warped, or water-logged are common in beginning classes and do serious damage to the development of good embouchure habits. The instructor should observe his students as they assemble their instruments, and he should conduct occasional unannounced reed inspections.

The single reed should be placed on the mouthpiece so that a hairline of reed shows above the tip of the mouthpiece (to allow the reed to curve against the face of the mouthpiece). Ligatures should be adjusted so that the upper edge of the ligature is in line with the bottom of the scrape of the reed *and* the bottom of the window in the mouthpiece. Many mouthpieces are scribed with lines to indicate ligature position.

All reeds should be kept in ventilated protective cases when not in use. They should also be protected from careless handling in the classroom. The teacher should encourage students to keep reeds away from their clothing.

13

The
Brasswind
Instruments

All brasswind instruments, regardless of the course of their development, work on the same basic principles. In their simplest forms the brasswinds are lengths of tubing, partly cylindrical and partly conical, with a cup-shaped mouthpiece at one end and a flaring bell at the other. The tone-generating mechanism is the center of the player's lips vibrating as a stream of air is forced between them.

The fundamental principle of the brasswinds can be demonstrated readily by inserting a cup-shaped mouthpiece in one end of a four- or five-foot length of garden hose and a funnel at the other. This "instrument" will produce a distinctive sound no matter how it is bent, and its pitch will be determined by its length. All brass instruments are essentially simple tubes of the proper length and diameter to provide for pitch and quality, but bent into distinctive shapes to make them easy to handle.

THE HARMONIC SERIES

Brass instruments produce a fundamental tone when the air column vibrates in one part. By increasing the speed of the air column, tightening the lip muscles, and increasing the pressure of the mouthpiece on the lips, the column of air may be made to vibrate in parts, referred to as "harmonics," "partials," or "overtones"—terms that are not truly synonymous as the chart below indicates.

Harmonics Partials	1	2	3	4	5	6	7	8	9	10	11	12	13	14	15	16
Overtones		1	2	3	4	5	6	7	8	9	10	11	12	13	14	15

A bugle, the least complex of the brass instruments, uses the first five overtones. The other brasses normally go considerably higher in the series (to the 8th, 9th, or 10th for cornet, trombone, etc.; to the 16th for the French horn). The fundamental is quite difficult to produce and is used only for special effects.

THE VALVE SYSTEM

Until the perfection of valves in the first quarter of the nineteenth century, only the notes of the harmonic series were available, and players could change keys only by using instruments of different sizes or by adding crooks or slides. Horn players could produce diatonic and some chromatic intervals by inserting the right hand into the bell of the instrument. This accounts for the writing of brass parts designated by keys, a tradition that has persisted. With the adoption of valves, the full chromatic possibilities of the instruments were made available. The valves serve to bridge the gaps between the "open" tones of the overtone series by lengthening the tubing. The same effect is procurable on the trombone by extending the slide.

Since there are seven chromatic steps to be accounted for between the second and third tones of the harmonic series, the valves are designed to be used singly or in combination to produce the half steps. There are the same number of valve combinations as there are trombone positions.

Trombone Positions	Valve Combinations	
1	0	Any partial of the harmonic series
2	2	Semi-tone (½ step) lower
3	1	Major second (1 step) lower
4	1-2	Minor third (1½ step) lower
5	2-3	Major third (2 steps) lower
6	1-3	Perfect fourth (2½ steps) lower
7	1-2-3	Augmented fourth (3 steps) lower

None of the valve *combinations* can be perfectly in tune with the equally-tempered chromatic scale. Equal temperament depends upon a fixed ratio of one tone to the next (1:1.05945+). Since the length of valve tubing is fixed, combinations are too short. For this reason extra triggers and movable slides are found on many brass instruments. Beginning students must be taught that their instruments are not perfect and that they must listen to every tone and adjust the pitch by changing the amount of lip tension. This is the basis for the very important admonition that brass players must sing before they play. Once they have their ears "set" through singing and listening they are more likely to play in tune.

The trombone is perhaps the easiest of the brasses to play in tune, since a minute adjustment of the slide can correct most deficiencies. However, the problems of teaching beginners to play in tune are akin to those of teaching string players—approximate positions may be indicated by the teacher, but it is the student's ear that must be the final guide. The intonation problems of valve and slide instruments can only be solved to the extent that young students learn to apprehend music through the ears; hence the rationale for beginning instruction by rote methods.

ASSEMBLING
BRASSWIND INSTRUMENTS

Putting a brass instrument together is much easier than assembling a woodwind instrument, but every bit as much care is required. All the brasses require the insertion of the mouthpiece into the blowpipe. This must be demonstrated so that students realize that it is to be done with a *slight* downward and twisting motion. The instructor must insist that the mouthpiece never be struck or slapped so that it sticks in the blowpipe.

A stuck mouthpiece may occur at any time. Students should be instructed that home repairs are *never* to be made. The well-intentioned father, working without the proper tools and techniques, can easily turn a simple and inexpensive job into a major and expensive overhauling. An amateur repairman, unaware of the thinness of the brass and how much pressure he can exert with pliers, can twist the blowpipe like a paper straw and perhaps tear loose the soft-soldered braces in the bargain. The instructor of a beginning class should have a mouthpiece puller available so that the stuck mouthpiece may be pulled straight out of the blowpipe without any twisting motion. Students should be told to bring an instrument with a stuck mouthpiece to the next class meeting, even if it means carrying the instrument out of the case.

It is important to remember that the brass in a brass instrument is very thin and very vulnerable to denting. Students should be told to handle the instruments with great care and to avoid putting books and other articles in the instrument cases.

CARE OF
BRASSWIND INSTRUMENTS

The brasswind instruments require considerably less care than do woodwind instruments because they have fewer moving parts. But unfortunately, even the simplest of instruments is vulnerable to inept handling.

When a brass instrument does not respond and air cannot be blown through it, the air passage is blocked in one of three ways: A valve has been turned around in its casing so that the ports are not aligned with the valve slide openings, a valve has been replaced in the wrong casing, or extraneous matter has become stuck in the mouthpiece or the tubing.

All valves have guides that hold them in proper alignment with the slide openings. If there is only one guide, there can be no possibility of error unless the valve is forced into the casing without lining up the guide with the slot in which it runs. However, many instruments have two or three guides. A quick examination of the guides and the key-ways inside the casing will usually enable correction of the error.

Most valves are stamped with the number of the casing into which they fit. Sometimes these numbers appear on the valve stems, sometimes they are stamped or scratched on the under surface of the valve caps. Valve #1 will not work properly in casing #2 or casing #3 although it might slide up and down.

If the valves have been discovered to be correctly in place, the obstruction in the tubing may be found by blowing through separate sections of the tubing. It is best to start with the mouthpiece, then the blowpipe with the tuning slide removed, since these are the locations most likely to be obstructed. If the obstruction is in the mouthpiece or blowpipe, it may be pushed out with a flexible cleaning brush. Obstructions in other parts of the tubing are rare, but occasionally the bell will be stopped up. Obstructions in the bell should be removed only by a competent repairman.

Fuzzy, breathy tones are usually the result of leaks in the tubing. These are most likely to occur when the water-key cork is broken or missing, when the water-key spring is too weak or is broken, or when the screw holding the water-key has become loose. Replacing a loose water-key screw is not difficult, but most other repairs should be done by professionals. If the fuzzy tone persists after the water-key has been repaired, the tightness of all tubing joints should be checked. These joints sometimes are weakened when valve tubes are bent to the side by books or other articles in instrument cases.

The conscientious teacher will spend some time (after students have met with some success in playing their instruments) showing his students how to care for their instruments. He will also conduct periodic instrument inspections. Students should be instructed to rinse out their mouths if they are going to play after eating. Food particles are easily carried into the instrument where they lodge, decay, and cause foul odors. Mouthpieces and blowpipes can become partially blocked with this kind of debris. Frequent cleaning of the mouthpiece with a cone-shaped mouthpiece brush and of the blowpipe with a flexible cleaning brush will prevent the collection of dirt.

From time to time, a brass instrument (*never, never* a woodwind) should be flushed out with lukewarm water (never hot water). The water is allowed to run into the bell until the stream comes out the blowpipe. Then one valve at a time is depressed so that the valve tubing is also flushed. The water should be shaken and blown out of the instrument. If the valve tubes are removed to clear them of water, the inner, fixed tubes should be wiped clean with a lint-free cloth and lubricated with valve grease or petroleum jelly.

The heart of a valve instrument is the set of valves in their casings. These are sliding mechanisms and must be manufactured to very fine tolerances in order to prevent the leakage of air. Piston valves should be removed, cleaned, oiled, and returned to their casings *one at a time* to prevent their transposition into the wrong casing. They must be handled with extreme care, since a very small dent will prevent their smooth movement in the casing. Students should be warned never to try to put a valve back in its casing after it has been dropped or dented since it may stick fast or damage the inner surface of the casing. Oiling can usually be done without taking valves from their casings by pulling them, one at a time, and gently, about half-way out of the casings, applying two drops of oil, and gently lowering them back to position. This can be done readily by unscrewing the top valve cap and pulling valve and cap straight up.

Valves may be cleaned with a lint-free cloth. The inner surface of the casing may be cleaned by removing the bottom cap, rolling a cloth into a cigar-like roll, and pushing it through the casings. If metal cleaning rods are used, the cloth should be wrapped completely around the rod so that the interior of the casing cannot be scratched.

The rotary valves of French horns are the most delicate of all the brass instrument mechanisms. The valve itself should never be removed by the student (nor by teachers not thoroughly knowledgeable). Oiling may be done by removing the valve cap and placing a single drop of oil on the axle. A drop of oil on the valve shaft opposite the cap is also recommended. If additional oiling is necessary, a drop or two may be placed in the valve crook. When the crook is replaced, the oil will work its way into the valve and the casing.

Only the finest valve oil should be used. Under no circumstances should household oil or trombone oil be used for they are too thick and cause sluggish action. Nor should water be used as a valve lubricant because it contains chemicals that may corrode the plating on the valve and casing surfaces.

The alignment of valve ports with valve tubing is affected by the thickness of the cork washers. Adjustment of these washers should be entrusted only to an experienced repairman.

Trombone slides are particularly vulnerable to twisting motions, side pressures, and dents. The tolerances are usually so small that the slightest nick in the outer slide will cause binding. Warped slides, caused by careless handling in assembly or pressure from books carried in cases, also bind. Only skilled repairmen with fine equipment can correct faulty slides.

In caring for the trombone, the student should hold the instrument perpendicularly to the floor and carefully remove the outer slide, putting it aside on a flat surface. The inner slide is then wiped clean with a lint-free cloth. Slide oil (not valve or domestic oil) is placed on the stockings at the ends of the inner slides and the outer slide is replaced, again with the instrument in a vertical position.

Most modern brasswind instruments are covered with lacquer or are plated with silver. Either finish can be kept clean if it is regularly wiped with a damp cloth. Silver-plated instruments tarnish easily and will need to be polished with a silver cleaner occasionally. Only a good grade of cleaner should be used, and it should be applied sparingly.

Emergency repairs in the brasswinds are usually limited to the replacement of a broken French horn string. The threading is not difficult if one begins with a string knotted at one end and then follows the path indicated by the unbroken strings. String tension is set by the small screw on the end of the lever; valve position is set by the small screw near the valve axle.

EMBOUCHURE FORMATION
AND MOUTHPIECE
PLACEMENT

Students selected to play brass-wind instruments should have straight teeth and an average overbite. Crooked teeth will lead to discomfort and often cause a player to place the mouthpiece at an incorrect spot on his lips.

Every brasswind teacher has his own theory of embouchure formation, and there is considerable disagreement about what constitutes a correct embouchure and how it is to be taught. Many teachers believe that beginning students either have or have not a natural embouchure for the brass instruments—and that a student who does not possess the natural embouchure should play a woodwind, stringed, or percussion instrument. Therefore, potential brasswind students should be tested with the mouthpiece or with the instrument before a final decision on the choice of instrument is made.

Generally speaking, the embouchure for a brasswind instrument is formed by (1) pointing the chin downward so that the flesh of the chin is drawn taut, (2) forming a puckered smile with the lips together, and (3) keeping the corners of the mouth firm.

The mouthpiece should be placed exactly in the center of the puckered smile. Most teachers agree that the French horn mouthpiece must be placed so that about two-thirds of its circumference rests on the upper lip and that the mouthpieces of other brass instruments are placed so that their circumferences are about equally divided between upper and lower lips. In actual practice, the setting of the mouthpiece is usually determined by the results obtained.

Once the mouthpiece is properly placed on the lips, the student should blow easily until the lips begin to vibrate. Some teachers ask their students to "buzz" the lips first. Others feel that "buzzing" without the mouthpiece creates undue tenseness and that the lips will vibrate more naturally if they do so against the resistance of the mouthpiece. When the student has produced a sound with the lips in the mouthpiece and has shown that he can sustain the sound, the mouthpiece may be placed in the instrument and the first tone attempted.

Some teachers believe that the most difficult embouchure to develop is that of the cornet and trumpet. These teachers select cornet and trumpet students according to their ability to produce a natural tone on the mouthpiece at the very earliest trials. Those who have difficulty are

57941

asked to try another brass instrument. Many teachers have learned that although a person might have difficulty producing the higher tones on a cornet or trumpet, he might be very successful on the wider cups of baritone, trombone, or tuba, or the deeper cup of the French horn. It is generally accepted that the embouchure is somewhat looser for the larger cups of the lower brass instruments.

TONGUING ON
BRASSWIND INSTRUMENTS

As with the woodwind instruments, the tongue acts as a valve to release air from the lungs into the instrument. Actual tongue placement and movement will vary slightly from instrument to instrument. In cornet, trumpet, and horn playing, the tongue is usually placed behind the upper teeth, where the teeth and gum meet. For the larger brass instruments, the tongue is brought down. Bass players will perhaps tongue between the teeth; some have been known to anchor the tongue against the lower teeth and let the middle of the tongue strike against the upper teeth.

14

The
Percussion
Instruments

Percussion instrument players may be started readily in elementary schools. Usually beginners take their first instruction on the snare drum and advance to the other percussion instruments—bass drum, timpani, cymbals, the various accessories, and the melodic percussion. Beginning students should use practice pads at home and at their lessons. Besides being less expensive than drums, they are much quieter and crisper in their response. Practice pads should always be provided with adjustable stands so that beginners will not learn incorrect positions by having to reach up to a table top or down to the seat of a chair.

A great variety of sizes, shapes, and weights of snare drum sticks is available. Beginners should use sticks of medium weight, thickness, and length. The student should learn to select pairs of sticks that are balanced and straight. Balance may be tested by listening to the pitch of the sticks as they are tapped lightly against a hard surface; straightness may be tested by rolling the sticks on a flat surface.

SNARE DRUM STICK POSITION

In snare drum playing, the two hands are held in different positions. This is because of the early use of the snare drum in marching units, where it was found that the instruments were easier to carry and play if the drum heads were at an angle with the left side higher than the right. The hand position has become traditional and persists even in non-marching performance and in spite of recent attempts to make all stick-holding uniform.

The left hand position may be acquired by holding the left hand parallel to the floor, palm down, with the fingers together and the thumb extended. The drum stick is placed in the webbing between the thumb and the index finger with the butt end of the stick protruding above the hand for about one-third of the length of the stick. The thumb is then brought over to the index finger to hold the stick securely, and the hand is turned over with an outward motion of about 135 degrees. As the hand is rotated, the little finger and the ring finger are curved over close to the palm of the hand in a relaxed manner under the stick. The index and middle fingers curve slightly toward the stick but do not lock themselves firmly on the stick.

The right hand position may be acquired by placing the stick on a table with the butt of the stick extending over the table's edge. The stick is grasped at a point about one-third of its length from the butt as if "shaking hands with it." The weight of the stick is supported by the thumb and the second joint of the index finger, which provide a pivot for the movement of the stick.

Practice should begin with one hand alone. The right hand "waves" up and down, the wrist being kept relaxed. Students must be cautioned not to play with a movement of the forearm from the elbow, although there is some residual motion there. The principal movement must come from the wrist. When the stick strikes the drum head or the practice pad, the wrist must snap it away as if the hand were recoiling from touching a hot surface. All right hand strokes must be in exact rhythm, of the same intensity, and strike the practice pad exactly in its center.

When right hand movement has become fairly secure, work on the left hand should begin. Here the movement involves a *turning* of the left forearm. The wrist does not move back and forth, and the arm does not move up and down. To start the stroke, the bead of the stick should be placed on the pad. The forearm is then turned backwards and brought rapidly toward the pad. It is often wise to practice one stroke at a time in the early stages. Once the movement seems to be fairly well understood, repeated quarter notes may be played, with care that they are even in rhythm and intensity and that the bead always strikes the same spot on the pad. Most students find control of the left stick much more difficult to acquire than control of the right stick and will drop the left stick frequently until the grip has been mastered. Because of this, many teachers prefer to begin work with the left hand strokes.

When single strokes are under control, the student progresses to series of four taps with the right hand followed by four taps with the left hand, in rhythm. The sticks should both strike the same general area of the pad. The teacher will need to be alert for the tendency of young students to move the shoulders toward the pad in sympathy with the movement of the hand. The four-tap series can be followed by a series of three strokes, then two strokes, until facility enables alternating hand-to-hand single strokes. This routine should be reviewed at every lesson for several weeks.

After the student has achieved reasonable security in hand-to-hand taps, he should be routined in combinations of 3, 5, 7, and 9 taps in this manner:

Each combination is to be practiced separately until it is mastered. When the student has become proficient, he should be able to change from one pattern to another as his instructor asks.

These routines are important because they not only develop the necessary elements for proper sticking but also lay the foundation for rolls produced by rebounding. With a little extra pressure on the bead of the stick, a stroke can be made to bounce so that there are two separate attacks. When the earlier combinations are permitted to rebound they produce rolls:

Rebounding of 4, 6, or 8 taps can lead to the development of 7-stroke, 11-stroke, and 15-stroke rolls.

These fundamental routines should be augmented by reading material playable with single strokes, and the student should be permitted to play on a snare drum from time to time. The drum head should be struck between the rim and the center—never *in* the center, as the sound will be "dead." Beginners will enjoy doing all these routines to the sound of phonograph records and will benefit from the experience of maintaining steady tempos.

Students will also profit from an occasional experience with the bass drum after they have learned to play the parts on practice pads. The bass drum must be struck at a point about half-way between the center and the rim. To reduce the rumble of a bass drum, the player may rest his idle hand against the head not being struck.

Teachers should try to help students learn that percussion instruments are to be *played*, not *hit*. The ideal might be expressed as drawing music *out* of the drum rather than pounding it *in*. Percussion students should be selected for their attentiveness, success in academic class work, and fine sense of rhythm. Since the percussion instruments can create a stronger rhythmic effect than any other group in a band or orchestra, the teacher should be very careful in selecting and grooming the drummers. A background in piano will be very helpful to the percussionist who is to play the melodic percussion instruments. Students with pianistic facility should be encouraged to play bells, marimba, and timpani as soon as possible to heighten their interest. The accessories and Latin-American instruments will also stimulate and maintain the enthusiasm of young percussionists.

15

Instrumental Music in American Public Schools Today

The United States moves into the last third of the twentieth century in the midst of a great cultural boom. Conditions have never been as favorable for the arts as they are at this time. Huge sums of money are being expended for arts centers in cities and on college campuses. Amateur and professional orchestras and singing groups abound as never before. Major productions in music, drama, and dance, formerly presented almost exclusively in large metropolitan areas, are now staged throughout the land. Reproductions of the paintings and sculptures of masters are available to all.

The work accomplished in public schools in the first sixty years of the century has stimulated much of the great interest now enjoyed by the arts. No longer considered frills upon the fabric of American life, the arts have been accepted, by most people, as important in the general culture of the nation's children.

AMERICAN MUSICIANS FROM AMERICAN SCHOOLS

In the nineteenth century most of the professional musicians working in the United States had been trained in Europe. Most American musicians of the 1960's, amateur and professional, started their training in the public elementary schools. They continued their training in junior and senior high schools through class instruction and participation in various ensembles. Those with special interests and skills supplemented their training with intensive private study. However, the great American system of teaching musical instruments in classes—unique to America and only about fifty years old—has probably helped more than any other factor to produce the abundance of music practitioners and consumers in this country at the moment. The system has done its work efficiently, economically, and democratically.

Private teachers have played an important role in the development of instrumental music in American schools. Through their efforts, students who first experienced instrumental music in classes have been able to continue their musical growth to the highest possible level. Private teachers have contributed to every exceptional instrumental music program by providing a specialized kind of instruction and inspiration available only in the highly individualized private lesson.

Increasingly, the roster of private teachers has come to include those who, like their students, are products of the public school instrumental music class.

IMPROVEMENT IN THE STATUS OF INSTRUMENTAL MUSIC TEACHERS

Teachers of instrumental music have found increasing acceptance of the importance of their work. When instrumental music was first taught in public schools, teachers were either supernumeraries teaching on a fee basis or teachers of other subjects who taught instrumental music classes before and after school or on Saturdays. Today's instrumental music teachers form, for the most part, integral parts of the school's professional staff with salaries, privileges, and responsibilities commensurate with those of the teachers of the older "academic" subjects. Fewer and fewer schools charge extra fees for instrumental music and some states have, by law or the interpretation of law, prohibited the assessment of fees for membership in instrumental music classes.

In the early years of the school band movement a band director would sometimes undertake to teach students at their own expense and to provide a school band if he could use school facilities without charge. Such a director would accrue much of his income from commissions received from the sale of instruments to his students. These practices have been practically eliminated, as they should be, for no public school teacher should profit at the expense of his students if he is to be professional in the truest sense.

The first school bands were extracurricular organizations. Rehearsals and beginning classes were rarely scheduled during the regular hours of school. Today, especially in secondary schools, instrumental music is scheduled with at least as much care as is given to other classes. Scheduling still depends upon the needs and philosophies of individual school systems, so that there is no unanimity of scheduling practices—but instrumental music is no longer a curricular stepchild.

Since the end of World War II, and particularly since the first Russian missile flight in 1957, the curriculum of the elementary school has expanded greatly. Existing programs have been intensified and additional personnel provided. Schools that once were served only by visiting teachers of music and art, and, sometimes, a school nurse, must now find room and time for visiting teachers of conversational foreign languages, physical education, and mathematics. Psychologists, psychometrists, speech correctionists, and others also provide highly specialized services that make demands on space and time. Since music competes with all these courses and services, the instrumental music teacher must be vigorous in the pursuit of more effective scheduling practices and space allocations.

The giving of credit for instrumental music in secondary schools is now common. However, not all schools give instrumental music courses credit equal to that granted for other subjects, nor do all schools giving credit allow four years of such credit to apply toward graduation requirements. Thus, instrumental music in some secondary schools remains as part of the extracurriculum.

WIDE DIVERSITY IN INSTRUMENTAL MUSIC OFFERINGS

While instrumental music has made significant progress, vast differences in the quality and quantity of music programs exist from state to state, from city to city, and even among schools in a single city. These differences are by-products of the organization of the American public school system.

Currently in the United States there are approximately 29,000 autonomous school districts. Members of the governing boards of these districts are selected in a variety of ways. Some are appointed by elected officials; others are elected on a partisan basis; most are elected in non-partisan elections either as representatives of the community at large or as representatives of wards or other political subdivisions. The "mix" of school board members, consequently, varies greatly and is constantly changing in every community. Some boards consist almost entirely of professional people interested in community service. Others include people with a number of special and perhaps limited points of view. A board of education is charged, by law and tradition, with the responsibility of providing schools, teachers, administrators, and facilities for the education of the children of the community.

A school board hires, as its chief administrative officer, a superintendent of schools. Some boards then delegate all responsibility to the superintendent and his staff, reserving for the board the role of watchdog and usually supporting the action of the professional educators. Other boards play a far more active role, determining policy, regulating course offerings (and even course content at times), participating in the selection of personnel and materials, and using the professional staff as a body of employees to carry out their wishes.

Within any school system, no matter what kind of control is exercised by the board of education, differences in school constituencies, the philosophies of principals, and the availability of facilities will affect the curriculum and schedule of individual schools.

The presence, the quantity, and the quality of instrumental music in a school, then, are determined by many factors. The success of a program of instrumental music depends to a great degree on the ability of the professional staff of music teachers to assess the needs and resources of the community and to maintain liaison with administrators, board members, and patrons so that their recommendations will be heard.

The democratic control of education as exemplified by the American system enables the citizens whose children are being educated to have a voice in the control of that education. A recurrent phenomenon is the emergence of factions demanding improvements, or at least changes, in curricula. As of the middle 1960's some of these demands were for more or better courses in mathematics, the sciences, and foreign languages. As these demands are met, other portions of the curriculum will come under scrutiny. While certain aspects of the system cause unhappiness and even dismay at times, the basic premise is sound and has resulted in a steady elevation of goals and achievements in public education.

In spite of the differences in quality and quantity of instrumental music instruction, teachers of instrumental music have achieved much. Many school bands and orchestras play fine music in a manner that closely matches the style of professional musicians. Most of the credit goes to the teachers themselves, not only for the missionary work of the early years but for the eagerness of teachers to join together in state and national organizations to improve the quality of music and music teaching. Instrumental music teachers as a group have grown professionally since the years after World War I. Their first organization, the National School Band Association, was formed primarily to enable participants at national contests to benefit from reduced railroad fares. Today's associations are concerned with philosophies, methodologies, and improved liaison with other educational groups. Where once band directors were interested only in building bigger and better bands regardless of the consequences to the total education of their students, teachers of the 1960's consider instrumental music an important part of total education—one that must not intrude on other parts. Once the emphasis was on the entertaining and social aspects of the school's band; today it is on music as a cultural achievement in the history of man. Once it was enough merely to teach a child to play an instrument; now the child is to have a chance to study great musical literature as well as musical theory so that he will have something to carry with him after graduation if he no longer cares to play.

ADDITIONAL DEVELOPMENTS

As state and national associations of music teachers have become more influential, they have tended to develop subgroups, study committees, and workshops. These smaller bodies have been the prime movers in the creation of music theory workbooks to be used by students in instrumental music classes; in the development of plans and devices to teach music literature through the study and performance of a basic repertoire covering all periods and styles; in the stimulation of solo performance through proficiency examinations beyond the limits of solo competition; and in the search for other means of making participation in instrumental music of greater value to the student.

Larger and more forward-looking schools are offering class piano, class voice, music theory, music appreciation, music history, private lessons for credit, general music, conducting, small ensembles, and recreational music. Smaller schools, with less affluent constituencies, often provide at least some of these services to their students. Many high schools are developing humanities courses utilizing team-teaching of English, social studies, art, and music.

THE MUSIC EDUCATOR AND
THE PROFESSIONAL MUSICIAN

Until recent years professional music and school music were worlds apart. Men in major symphony orchestras, studio and conservatory teachers, and soloists were almost exclusively born and trained in Europe, performed the music of European composers, and perpetuated the European musical tradition. Teachers of music in the schools were, for the most part, born and raised in America, although their musical diet was necessarily European. The two worlds have grown closer and closer together.

In the twentieth century the professional musician has supplemented his income by teaching American students in such schools and conservatories as the Curtis Institute of Music, the Juilliard School of Music, and the Eastman School of Music. Other professional musicians have found teaching positions in the music departments of major colleges and universities, where they, too, have come to know American students, trained in American schools.

The result of this interchange has been better teaching of college students, many of whom have gone into professional music or into teaching. Those who have chosen to become teachers in the public schools have helped to raise the standards of teaching and performance by providing better and more meaningful instruction.

In recent years public school music teachers, through their professional associations, and often with the aid of generous financial support from the music industry, have obtained the services of professional musicians to conduct clinics, workshops, and demonstrations on the various instruments. Such meetings have increased the flow of ideas. The music educator has learned much from the professional, and the professional has become more sympathetic toward school music.

Although most of America's professional musicians are now products of the public school system, the nation is just beginning to produce and recognize its conductors and composers. Financial grants by the Ford Foundation for the development of American composers and conductors have been of great importance. However, composers still have difficulty in securing performances of their works, and conductors still find it almost impossible to find ensembles to conduct unless they go to Europe.

WITH PROPER GOALS, A BRIGHT FUTURE

Music has achieved a strong and unique place in American public schools. The advancement has been made in a relatively few years. What, however, are the present goals in music education? What is the purpose of music in the schools? And what are teachers *really* trying to accomplish? Basically, the goals are what they were when Lowell Mason brought the singing-school to the school houses of Boston over a century ago—the development of a love and understanding of music.

Paul van Bodegraven, president of the Music Educators National Conference in 1964–66, states the position in this way: "The common objectives of music teaching at all levels of instruction are: (1) to foster growth in the understanding of music, and (2) to develop a sense of discrimination in dealing with it. These objectives are precise and specific and can be readily converted into action in all phases of the music program." [1]

Allen P. Britton, president of the Conference in 1960–62, summed up the present status of music education succinctly. "Of greatest significance, perhaps, is the simple fact that education in music is not very new in our country, as seems to be the general opinion; that, on the contrary, instruction in music has always been a part of our educational systems. Our musical heritage is rich rather than poor. Thus, we probably have no need to be overanxious about the future of music education here, nor do we need to be unduly apologetic in our insistence that music continue to occupy an important place in education. Given our historical background, there is no reason to fear that Americans may suddenly forget their love of music nor that they may suddenly seek to remove it from the education of their children." [2]

While it is true that technological achievements and social changes may create a need for alterations in our curricula, and that various local and state legislative bodies may make decisions affecting the curricula, it is doubtful that any significant event will take place in the immediate future that will permanently eliminate the teaching of music in the schools. In fact, the future for the arts has never been as hopeful, and the young teacher today can look forward to a rich and rewarding career. The path will often be strewn with obstacles, but these will be minor irritants to one whose objectives include the provision of an honest education in music for the children of America.

[1] "Music Education in Transition," *Music Educators Journal,* LI (June-July, 1965), p. 28.
[2] "Music in Early American Public Education: A Historical Critique," in *Basic Concepts in Music Education,* 57th Yearbook of the National Society for the Study of Education (Chicago: University of Chicago Press, 1958), p. 207.

Additional Readings

Andrews, Frances M. and Clara E. Cockerill, *Your School Music Program.* Englewood Cliffs, N.J.: Prentice-Hall, Inc., 1958.

Band and Orchestra Handbook, Elkhart, Ind.: Pan-American Band Instrument Division of C. G. Conn, Ltd., 1951.

Bartlett, Harry R., *Guide to Teaching Percussion.* Dubuque, Iowa: William C. Brown Company, 1964.

Buggert, Robert, *Teaching Techniques for the Percussion.* Rockville Centre, N.Y.: Belwin, Inc., 1961.

Collins, Myron D. and John E. Green, *Playing and Teaching Percussion Instruments.* Englewood Cliffs, N.J.: Prentice-Hall, Inc., 1962.

Farkas, Philip, *The Art of Brass Playing.* Bloomington, Ill.: Brass Publications, 1962.

————, *The Art of French Horn Playing.* Evanston, Ill.: Summy-Birchard Company, 1958.

Harris, Dale and Fred Wiest, *The Basic Method for Beginning Band.* New York: Educational Music Service, Inc., 1957.

Henry, Nelson B. (ed.), *Basic Concepts in Music Education,* Fifty-seventh Yearbook of the Society for the Study of Education, Part I. Chicago: University of Chicago Press, 1958.

House, Robert, *Instrumental Music for Today's Schools*. Englewood Cliffs, N.J.: Prentice-Hall, Inc., 1965.

Hovey, Nilo W., *The Administration of School Instrumental Music*. Rockville Centre, N.Y.: Belwin, Inc., 1952.

Kleinhammer, Edward, *The Art of Trombone Playing*. Evanston, Ill.: Summy-Birchard Company, 1963.

Kuhn, Wolfgang E., *Instrumental Music: Principles and Methods of Instruction*. Boston: Allyn and Bacon, Inc., 1962.

Leonhard, Charles and Robert W. House, *Foundations and Principles of Music Education*. New York: McGraw-Hill Book Company, 1959.

Maddy, J. E. and T. P. Giddings, *Instrumental Class Teaching*. Cincinnati: The Willis Music Company, 1928.

Mursell, James L., *Music Education: Principles and Programs*. Morristown, N.J.: Silver Burdett Company, 1956.

———— and Mabelle Glenn, *The Psychology of School Music Teaching*. Morristown, N.J.: Silver Burdett Company, 1931.

Normann, Theodore F., *Instrumental Music in the Public Schools*. Bryn Mawr, Pa.: Oliver Ditson Company, 1939.

Palmer, Harold G., *Teaching Techniques of the Woodwinds*. Rockville Centre, N.Y.: Belwin, Inc., 1952.

Prescott, Gerald R. and Lawrence W. Chidester, *Getting Results with School Bands*. New York: Carl Fischer, Inc., and Minneapolis: Paul A. Schmitt Music Co., 1938.

Righter, Charles Boardman, *Teaching Instrumental Music*. New York: Carl Fischer, Inc., 1959.

Sawhill, Clarence and Bertram McGarrity, *Playing and Teaching Woodwind Instruments*. Englewood Cliffs, N.J.: Prentice-Hall, Inc., 1962.

Snyder, Keith D., *School Music Administration and Supervision*. Boston: Allyn and Bacon, Inc., 1959.

Spencer, William, *The Art of Bassoon Playing*. Evanston, Ill.: Summy-Birchard Company, 1958.

Sprenkle, Robert and David Ledet, *The Art of Oboe Playing*. Evanston, Ill.: Summy-Birchard Company, 1961.

Stein, Keith, *The Art of Clarinet Playing*. Evanston, Ill.: Summy-Birchard Company, 1958.

Stubbins, William H., *The Art of Clarinetistry*. Ann Arbor, Mich.: Ann Arbor Publishers, 1965.

Sweeney, Leslie, *Teaching Techniques for the Brasses*. Rockville Centre, N.Y.: Belwin, Inc., 1953.

Taylor, Maurice D., *Easy Steps to the Band*. New York: Mills Music, Inc., 1942.

Teal, Larry, *The Art of Saxophone Playing*. Evanston, Ill.: Summy-Birchard Company, 1963.

Timm, Everett L., *The Woodwinds*. Boston: Allyn and Bacon, Inc., 1964.

Westphal, Frederick W., *Guide to Teaching Woodwinds*. Dubuque, Iowa: William C. Brown Company, Inc., 1962.

Willaman, Robert, *The Clarinet and Clarinet Playing*. New York: Carl Fischer, Inc., 1954.

Winslow, Robert W. and John E. Green, *Playing and Teaching Brass Instruments*. Englewood Cliffs, N.J.: Prentice-Hall, Inc., 1961.

Index

Here is a detailed presentation of the elementary school instrumental music class—the foundation of the entire band program. The major part of the book is devoted to the mechanics of setting up classes, principles of instruction, scheduling, control, and evaluation. Those crucial areas so often left to trial and chance, such as effective classroom control and those very important first sessions which set the tone for the rest of the year, are given thorough and helpful attention. The authors present an analysis of organizational and teaching problems and suggest proven methods for their solution. The factors basic to successful instrumental music teaching are covered—organization, recruitment, presentation, discipline, evaluation of *both* the student and the teacher, and maintaining interest.

Three chapters deal specifically with the three main types of band instruments: the woodwinds, the brasswinds, and the percussion instruments. Emphasis is placed on the development of individual musicianship and mastery of the intellectual content of instrumental musical performance.

(Continued on back flap)